EQUIPPING GRADUATES

FOR

YOUTH MINISTRY

Sue Peat

EQUIPPING GRADUATES

FOR

YOUTH MINISTRY

YTC Press
www.ytcpress.com
Monograph Series

YTC Press

An imprint dedicated to research on Youth, Theology & Culture

First published in 2008 by

YTC Press, Cambridge, UK

– A Division of Youth Focus –

www.ytcpress.com

www.youthfocus.biz

ISBN: 978-1-84799-267-3

Copyright © 2008 by Sue Peat

Youth Focus

Youth Focus is a partnership dedicated to providing good quality resources for those involved in Christian youth ministry at an affordable price. We undertake this ministry by

- Training volunteer, part-time and full-time youth workers throughout the world through our accredited online Emerge Academy, www.emergeacademy.net
- Providing lecture resources (scripts, handouts and PowerPoint presentations) for those involved in teaching youth ministry and associated disciplines, www.youthfocus.biz
- Publishing books, with our YTC Imprint through www.lulu.com, on youth ministry, ecclesiology, cultural studies, theology, education and associated disciplines

Youth Focus is based in the UK but partners with organisations around the world.

For more information, please contact Steve Griffiths through steve@youthfocus.biz or go to the websites:

www.youthfocus.biz
www.emergeacademy.net
www.ytcpress.com

For June and Eric.

I'm thankful to you for everything and proud to be your daughter.

Contents

Acknowledgements   xi

Chapter One   Introduction   13

Chapter Two   Research Methodology   19

Chapter Three   The Cliff College Experience   23

Chapter Four   Full-time Church-based Youth Ministry   29

Chapter Five   Research Results and Analysis   35

Chapter Six   Conclusion and Recommendations   59

Appendix A   Focus Group Discussion Extracts   65

Appendix B   Questionnaire Results   73

Appendix C   Interview Transcripts   83

Bibliography   139

Diagrams and Charts

Fig. 1: Brierley's Relationship Triangle   32

Fig. 2: Vocational Paths taken by Cliff Graduates
         1996-2005   35

Fig. 3: Questionnaire 1 Results   36

Fig. 4: Absolute Research Findings in Relation to
         Graduate Employment   36

Fig. 5: Respondents' Previous Youth Ministry
         Experience   39

Fig. 6: Length of time Respondents were employed in
         their initial Youth Ministry Post   39

Fig. 7: Reasons for Youth Workers Leaving their Initial
         Post   40

Fig. 8: Number of Years Respondents Studied at Cliff
         College   42

Fig. 9: Respondents' Ratings of Cliff College as
         Preparation for Youth Ministry   43

Acknowledgements

The list of people I wish to thank seems endless. However, I would like to name a few:

All the Tutors and Evangelists at Cliff who have helped me, believed in me and encouraged me throughout the MA course upon which this book is based. In particular, I wish to thank Martyn Atkins, Pete Phillips, Steve Wild, Stephen Skuce, Helen Edwards and Eva Walker. In different ways, you have all been instrumental in me getting to this point.

I also wish to thank all the participants in the research, without whom this book would not have been possible. It is my hope and prayer that this research is influential in assisting future youth workers in the essential ministry amongst young people.

Finally, thanks to God, my constant source of inspiration, encouragement and vision. This has been a journey of discovery and one I am privileged to have taken.

In compliance with legal obligations, all information accessed from the Cliff database has been used only for the purpose of this research and respondents' details have remained anonymous.

Chapter One

Introduction

The last decade has seen an increase in the number of churches in the United Kingdom employing full-time youth workers. A recent study by the Church of England suggests that, 'the Church employs more youth workers than local government.'[1] A Church Life Profile undertaken in 2001 indicates that around one in six churches employs a youth worker, signalling a figure of approximately 6000 church-based youth workers in England, half of whom are full-time.[2] Conversely, the latest *Religious Trends* research shows that in England, between 1998 and 2005, the number of 11-19 year olds attending church fell by 22%.[3] Despite falling church attendance amongst young people, the growing number of full-time church-based youth workers suggests increased commitment to youth ministry.

[1] Board of Education and Board of Mission, *Good News for Young People: The Church of England's National Youth Strategy* (London: Archbishop's Council, 2002), p.1.
[2] Gelder A and Escott P, 'Profile of Youth Workers' in *Churches Together in England Co-ordinating Group for Youth Work* (London: Private Report, 2003), pp. 4-5.
[3] Brierley P (ed), *UK Christian Handbook Religious Trends No. 6* (Worcester: The Trinity Press, 2007), pp. 12.2-12.3.

Engaging in youth ministry is an exciting, challenging, rewarding and vital component of the Church's mission; it is simultaneously frustrating, demanding and exhausting. Generations of youth workers; Christian based and statutory, full-time and part-time, paid and voluntary, have attested to this. Young people are exploring and discovering much about themselves and the world around them; and experiencing crucial changes physically, emotionally, sexually and spiritually. It is a privilege to journey alongside young people, sharing in their pain and in their joy. The opportunity to point the way to Christ as the one who can make sense of life, through words, actions and steadfast commitment, comes with vast responsibility. This incarnational view of mission provides the foundation for this research.

Research Purpose

The purpose of this research is to analyse and evaluate the extent to which Cliff College graduates are prepared for youth ministry and the consequential impact this has upon the young people and churches concerned. This study indicates that, between 1996 and 2005, at least 19% of Cliff College graduates were employed by churches as full-time youth workers.[4] This research will enable Cliff (and, by extension, other colleges and seminaries) to better equip those entering youth ministry, alongside considering whether it is realistic for a Bible College to prepare graduates specifically for youth ministry.

I studied at Cliff from 1993-95 and subsequently was employed as a youth pastor. In many ways I felt unprepared and found aspects of the work testing. I returned to Cliff in 1999 to work as an Evangelist and, following my own experience of full-time church-based youth ministry, I have been concerned for graduates entering such work. The hypothesis of this research, which will be tested throughout, is that many graduates entering full-time youth ministry are insufficiently prepared or simply not suited for such positions. This has been suggested through discussion with graduates employed as youth workers, many of whom have had negative employment experiences. Several contracts have been prematurely terminated by the youth worker or the employer. This has resulted in the youth worker experiencing failure and stress and, the church, disappointment, requiring resolution concerning its work with young people.

This research is focussed between 1996 and 2005 due to significant academic developments at the college. University validation began in 1994, and 1996-97 was the first year students were accepted

---

[4] Database information and Personal knowledge – see Chapter 5.1, p.28, Figure 4, p.29 and Questionnaire 1 Results, Appendix B, pp.75-76.

for a BA in Biblical and Evangelistic Ministry – validated by the University of Sheffield; the Level Three course initially ran in 1998-99. This period of nine years enabled focussed study and sufficiently varied responses for a good balance of data.

The outcome of this research will be to provide improved insight for colleges and seminaries in relation to the effectiveness of academic study, practical mission and placement experience, community life and tutorial contact in preparing graduates for youth ministry. It will offer improvements to supplement the preparation of graduates.

The results will be useful in highlighting negative and potentially damaging employment experiences; and as an aid to improve the equipping of students with the tools required to succeed as full-time youth workers, should that be their chosen vocation. This research has a wider scope too, as some of the findings will not be limited to youth workers. Improved insight into generic aspects of graduates' employment experiences will be helpful in preparing future students for varied vocations. It is my hope that graduates will enter positions of ministry sufficiently equipped, having a teachable character and the rudimentary skills required to engage in and develop such work.

Definition of Terms

'Graduates' refers specifically to those who studied full-time at Cliff College, and were 'leavers' between the years of 1996 and 2005 after one, two or three years of undergraduate study. This field is narrowed to graduates who within six months of leaving Cliff were employed as full-time, church-based youth workers, rather than undertaking further training or gaining significant further life experience. This is to ensure that, as far as possible, the research results will specifically relate to Cliff College as preparation for youth ministry and are not skewed by other factors.

Defining the term 'young people' is difficult. In the UK, young people are predominantly understood as those aged 11- 25,[5] although there is disagreement. The National Youth Agency (NYA), a UK government quango, defines the primary age of young people as 13-19[6], whilst many churches have a range of 11-18, or an upper age limit

---

[5] General Synod Working Party, *Youth A Part* (London: Church House Publishing, 1996), p.1.
[6] http://www.nya.org.uk/Templates/internal.asp?NodeID=90814 (National Youth Association website), accessed on 5 December 2006

as high as 26.[7] For the purpose of this research, 'youth' and 'young people' are to be understood as those aged between 13 and 19.

Full-time youth ministry, as opposed to part-time, will be examined due to significant distinctions pertinent to this research between these two spheres. The full-time youth worker is often under greater pressure from the church in relation to commitment, enthusiasm and vision for the work, as the employee usually has no other employment. Full-time youth workers often cite a specific calling to work full-time with young people, as opposed to part-time or volunteer work. Whilst many of the core values and motives for youth ministry remain the same throughout the continuum, it is the paid, full-time sector of youth ministry that will be examined.

I have elected to study only church-based youth ministry as opposed to other Christian youth work involving para-church organisations (PCOs). This is because organisations such as Youth for Christ (YFC) and Oasis provide employees with ongoing youth ministry training, where often churches do not. This distinction makes PCOs and churches less comparable and, therefore, should be evaluated separately.

Interestingly PCO graduates, despite their focussed training, are not immune to feeling under-prepared upon entering youth ministry. Pete Ward in *Growing up Evangelical*[8] reflects upon his involvement in training with Oxford Youth Works, acknowledging 'appointments did not always work out'[9] for graduates entering full-time church-based youth ministry.

Church-based youth ministry presents varied responsibilities from a broad spectrum of ministry. One youth worker within the Focus Group cited that she had not, 'fully appreciated how much other work within the church'[10] she was expected to do. This work incorporates generic aspects of ministry, such as liaising with church members, preaching, office administration, leadership meetings, and contact with parents. These additional responsibilities are important in the effectiveness of their work.

Youth Work or Youth Ministry?
This is a question debated amongst Christians in church-based and secular-based youth work. The term 'youth work' is generally accepted

---

[7] http://www.mayc.info/section.asp?id=1153 (MAYC Youth Conference 2006, Methodist Standing Order 250), accessed on 19 January 2007
[8] Ward P, *Growing up Evangelical* (London: SPCK, 1996)
[9] Ward, *Growing up Evangelical,* p.1.
[10] Focus Group Extracts, Appendix A, p.72.

within Local Education Authorities, whereas increasingly those involved in church-based youth work are adopting the term 'youth ministry' as a more accurate description.[11] Ward views the separation of the two terms as unhelpful, stating 'the use of the term youth ministry solely for work inside the Church and youth work for work outside the Church tends to perpetuate a sacred/secular divide.'[12]

Youth *work* should be incorporated into youth *ministry* and our understanding of the word 'ministry' broadened. Brierley, in *Joined Up*,[13] addresses this debate maintaining the importance of a continuing confluence of youth work and youth ministry, arguing 'for an end to the destructive duel between secular youth work and sacred youth ministry.'[14] I endorse Brierley's view that reconciling youth work and youth ministry as equal partners 'provides a genuinely holistic approach to working with young people,'[15] though for the purpose of this research, 'youth ministry' will be the term generally used. However, as many churches use the term 'youth work', some interview responses include this term. Those in full-time employment with churches are generally referred to as youth workers, thus the term used of the employee within this research is 'youth worker'.

Youth Ministry in the UK

The history of Christian youth ministry in the United Kingdom has been largely defined by the development of PCOs. In the nineteenth century, the Young Men's Christian Association (YMCA)[16] and Boys' Brigade were begun. More recently, YFC was introduced following the Billy Graham rallies in the 1950s.[17] This has been significant in its evangelistic influence upon young people.

The Church was at the forefront of work with young people for generations. However, a recent development is in churches employing a full-time worker specifically for the purpose of developing youth ministry. As the association of young people with the church has

---

[11] Ward P, *Youthwork and the Mission of God* (London: SPCK, 1997), p.4.

[12] Ward, *Youthwork*, p.4.

[13] Brierley D, *Joined Up* (Carlisle: Spring Harvest Publishing Division and Authentic Lifestyle, 2003)

[14] Brierley D, *Joined Up*, p.191.

[15] Brierley D, *Joined Up*, p.5.

[16] Ward P, 'Distance and Closeness: Finding the Right Ecclesial Context for Youthwork' in Ward P (ed) *The Church and Youth Ministry* (Oxford: Lynx Communications, 1995), pp.36-37.

[17] Ward, 'Distance and Closeness' in Ward (ed) *The Church and Youth Ministry*, p.37.

declined, youth ministry has become increasingly on the church's agenda. There is a vital need for mission and evangelism amongst young people through relevant and radical methods. The increased number of youth workers employed by churches suggests this commitment to young people is present. However, this could be contended by arguing that churches may be lacking in volunteer commitment to young people and thereby seek to employ specialists to do the work for them. From my engagement with this research over a significant period of time, I suggest that such cases are in a minority; churches today largely recognise the importance of long-term, contextualised ministry with young people, and are prepared to invest in such work, understanding youth ministry 'as a dimension of the Church's mission.'[18]

---

[18] General Synod Working Party, *Youth A Part,* p.23.

Chapter Two

Research Methodology

My concern for graduates entering youth ministry began in September 1999, although this was not formal or structured. I have become increasingly aware of graduates who, by their own admission, were not sufficiently prepared for posts. The research started in earnest in January 2005, following a structured plan and methodology.

Research was conducted through an initial focus group, questionnaires and one-to-one interviews, providing sufficient quantitative and qualitative results. This triangulation is likely to lead to valid and realistic information. To show the validity and the context of the research, a comprehensive survey of the vocational paths all graduates took within the timescale was required. With official support, information was accessed from the Cliff database, providing some details of graduate employment post-Cliff, and current contact details. This helped in narrowing the research group.

Focus Group
To assess the validity of the hypothesis and the potential merit of this research, a focus group was gathered at Cliff College, providing in-depth information from graduate youth workers. Such data was

important as the essence of successful or unsuccessful preparation for employment is difficult to quantify.

The Focus Group met in March 2005 and consisted of eight people: five Cliff graduates who left Cliff between 1996 and 2004, two Cliff students expressing an interest in youth ministry and myself as facilitator. There was a clear, though flexible, structure to the discussion. I was involved, though I deliberately withheld personal views to prevent directing other group members. The group discussed both positive and negative experiences; displaying enthusiasm and inspiration for youth ministry, alongside intelligently engaging with issues facing youth workers, particularly those in first appointments. The group affirmed the need for investigative study of the effectiveness of Cliff's full-time undergraduate course as preparation for youth ministry.

Questionnaires

Two questionnaires were used in the research. Questionnaire 1 was sent to the 74 graduates who were classified as 'unknowns' in terms of vocation paths after leaving Cliff, in order to determine their classification – 74% of which were returned. Questionnaire 2 went to the 40 graduates who were known to have entered youth ministry – 75% of which were returned. This provided a representative sample size, satisfying the demands of the statistical tests undertaken. The high return rate may be due to my personal knowledge of many of those contacted.

Questionnaire 2 considered aspects of youth ministry and the evaluation of the full-time undergraduate course at Cliff, which was more important to the research than Questionnaire 1 as it facilitated not only quantitative, but also qualitative evidence. A pilot study was carried out to assess the relevancy and wording of the questions, from which minor changes were made.

Interviews

Twelve formal interviews were conducted. Seven of these, selected from returned questionnaires, were graduates who had entered youth ministry within six months of graduating, one Cliff College course leader, two church leaders with experience in employing youth workers, one youth ministry specialist and one founder of an independent organisation involved in ongoing support of Bible College graduates. The interviews were semi-structured, allowing for elaboration and relevant digression, and facilitated a clear, balanced understanding of the research matter, providing helpful insight for subsequent analysis.

Reflexivity
The practice of reflexivity concerns 'critical self-scrutiny by the researcher.'[1] It is difficult for a researcher to be wholly neutral or detached from the information they generate.[2] Reflexivity requires the researcher to be 'self-aware of their own beliefs, values and attitudes, and their personal effects on the setting they have studied.'[3] This is of particular importance in qualitative research.[4]

Care was taken to enhance validity and reliability wherever possible throughout the research; potential bias is acknowledged however, due to my association with Cliff College throughout much of the period covered. In almost every case, those interviewed were personally known to me. This may have influenced their responses, despite my attempting to uphold professionalism as a researcher. In order to prevent potential bias marring the research, interviewees were encouraged to be honest in their responses and to include relevant criticisms. This had the desired effect, perhaps due to the fact that most of the interviewees had been disassociated with Cliff for over a year, enabling them to critically analyse their experiences objectively. Interviewees acknowledged the value of such research, thus were candid in their responses.

A reflective journal was kept throughout the research, recording observations and reactions. This aided self-awareness, and emphasised 'reflexivity as an intellectual resource, rather than a defensive audit.'[5]

---

[1] Mason J, *Qualitative Researching* (London: Sage Publications, 1996), p.5.
[2] Mason, *Qualitative Researching,* p.6.
[3] Payne G & Payne J, *Key Concepts in Social Research* (London: Sage Publications, 2005), p.191.
[4] Payne & Payne, *Key Concepts,* p.191.
[5] Payne & Payne, *Key Concepts,* p.192.

Chapter Three

The Cliff College Experience

'The charisms of Cliff College are focussed around a cluster of themes...evangelistic ministry, discipleship and formation for Christian ministry, evangelical theology, holiness and praxis as a process of teaching and learning.'[1]

These values form the foundation for all courses. Cliff College defines itself as 'a hybrid Bible College and Higher Education institution.'[2] Central motivations for studying at Cliff comprise increasing learning, including biblical, theological and sociological understanding; application of knowledge through practical experience; discussion of achievement, progress and future plans through tutorial contact and personal, spiritual and social development through community life. These features of Cliff College life are introduced here and examined within the Research Analysis in relation to their contribution to preparing students for youth ministry.

Academic Study

During 1996-2005, the actual content of the Cliff course has changed numerous times. Over a number of years, the course was refined and developed within the bounds of the new validation that began in 1994. The University of Sheffield accredited each graduate and they completed modules falling under the themes of Biblical Studies,

---

[1] *Collaborative Partner Report* (Cliff College: 2003), Section 2, p.1.
[2] *Collaborative Partner Report,* Section 2, p.3.

Christian and Social Studies and Evangelism and Ministry Skills,[3] which included both academic study and practical experience.

In the latter stages of the timescale, an optional module at Level Two entitled 'Evangelism and Young People'[4] was introduced, including 10 hours of lectures and 25 hours practical experience of youth ministry. This module takes the form of a weeklong placement, where students gain insight through academic study and discussion and then apply such learning through practical work. Whilst this module is helpful to students considering full-time youth ministry, it does not provide sufficient preparation, in itself, for such posts.

Cliff College has since transferred its academic validation to the University of Manchester. This shift wrought a change in the degree title from 'Bachelor of Arts (Hons) in Biblical and Evangelistic Ministry', which was alleged as being, 'easily misunderstood by prospective employers and other higher education institutions,'[5] to 'Bachelor of Arts (Hons) in Theology'. The narrower former title, of which most graduates within the time-frame of this research received, may have contributed to many entering church work without fully exploring other options.

In 2005, Cliff launched a new part-time undergraduate course entitled 'Diploma in Youth Mission and Ministry.'[6] Whilst this is relevant, it is a part-time course; it was introduced outside of the timeframe and as such does not come within the remit of this research.

Missions and Placements
'Cliff College could justly lay claim to be one of the foremost centres for the study of mission and evangelism in the United Kingdom.'[7] Commitment to mission and evangelism has been central to the ethos of Cliff since 1884,[8] and remains so today. Bosch defines mission as, 'the Church's participation in the work of the Spirit to renew the face of the earth'[9] involving, 'confronting the state with the claims of Christ's

---

[3] *Revalidation Portfolio* (Cliff College: 1999), E1-E14.

[4] *Evangelism and Young People Option Course Unit Outline* (Cliff College: 1999)

[5] *BA in Theology Course Approval Paperwork* (Cliff College: 2004), p.5.

[6] *Diploma in Youth Mission and Ministry Course Unit Outline* (Cliff College: 2004)

[7] *Revalidation Portfolio*, A31.

[8] *Collaborative Partner Report*, Section 2, p.1.

[9] Bosch D, 'Vision for Mission' in *International Review of Missions* LXXVI No 301, Jan 1987, p.14.

kingdom, calling it to be human, to treat all its citizens equally or, rather, to be biased towards the less privileged.'[10]

This view is intrinsic to Cliff's involvement in mission and evangelism though, here specifically, the practical outworking of mission implies set periods of time during which teams of students work in partnership with particular churches. In this context, mission can be expressed as working alongside Christian communities at the interface of the world and the Kingdom, contextualising the Gospel for those who have never heard.

The interrelationship of mission and evangelism is championed at Cliff. The ethos of missions is to, 'work with local churches in encouraging them to be evangelistic communities.'[11] This model of mission has been described as 'hit and run,'[12] short-term and in today's culture largely ineffective, but when proper partnerships are forged, it is often successfully provides moments of 'crisis' within ongoing mission.

During the research, depending on particular years of study, Level One students completed between 24 and 36 days of mission, Level Two students between 69 and 81 days and Level Three students between 42 and 56 days. Despite grasping in the lecture room the necessity of long-term, relational evangelism, much of this would have been church-based and event-focussed, even that termed 'placement' rather than mission. No student was able to specialise thus, while youth ministry may have featured for some, it will not have for others.

Phil Clarke, as Director of Evangelism, attempted to bring about more relational, long-term mission – though often these changes were thwarted. Clarke advocated a, 'change of mindset from mission as event to mission as the whole of life'[13] – Cliff's 'mission and placement practice must reflect this better.'[14] Students gain a range of experience in short-term mission but miss the crucial long-term relational emphases so essential in youth ministry.

For many years, a tension has existed in the practice of Cliff missions between providing excellence-resources for churches and providing training and experience for students. The former has the potential of resulting in students feeling stressed and under pressure to achieve; the key is in finding balance. The introduction of placements has allowed students to reflectively observe good practice, alongside

---

[10] Bosch, 'Vision for Mission' in *International Review of Missions,* p.14.
[11] Clarke P, *Together in Mission* (Calver: Cliff College Publishing, 1994), p.6.
[12] Clarke P, *Evangelism Report* (Cliff College: March 1999)
[13] Clarke, *Evangelism Report* (March 2000)
[14] Clarke, *Evangelism Report* (March 2000)

honing their own skills. The 'Evangelism Strategy', introduced in 2002/3, means students can now choose their own placements, either short-term or ongoing, enabling preparation for specific ministries after graduation.

Tutorial Contact

Race states that, 'the success of personal tutorial support is at best patchy. Some tutors take it very seriously...though for many students, their personal tutor is just a name.'[15] This is arguably not the case at Cliff College. Almost all Cliff tutors are ordained ministers with pastoral skills. Students are encouraged to seek counsel from tutors in relation to academic, personal and spiritual concerns. Most tutors live on site and are part of the community, leading house groups and involved in college life. Although some students invariably participate in more tutorial sessions, it is doubtful that any would claim that their tutor was 'just a name.'[16]

Students are assigned to a personal tutor, who is available for consultation at designated times each week; additional tutorials may also be arranged. Each year group has a Course Director, offering guidance particularly relevant to their overall course. The Dean of Students provides further support in matters of academic quality assurance, discipline and college management. Students receive formative assessment from tutors and appreciate the value of collegiality through small group tutorials; important for future ministries.

Tutorial contact plays an important role in vocational guidance. At Level Three, greater emphasis is placed upon discerning future careers and vocations. The potential careers scope for graduates is wide reaching; and, as noted by David Firth, Level Three Course Director, opens many paths, 'which can often provide more opportunities for evangelism than working in a church.'[17] Whilst careers' advice at Level Three is essential, such discussion should also be incorporated into Levels One and Two, enabling students to begin the discerning process much earlier.

Community Life

David Clarke identifies three features that combine to create community – 'a sense of solidarity, a sense of significance and a sense

---

[15] Race P, *The Lecturer's Tool Kit* (Abingdon: Routledge Falmer, 2004), pp.171-172.
[16] Race, *The Lecturer's Tool Kit*, p.172.
[17] David Firth Interview, Appendix C, p.121.

of security;'[18] features present at Cliff College. Most full-time students live on site and a large proportion of the Cliff experience centres on the college community. Often, God transforms students through the experience of life at Cliff. Close friendships and, indeed, dependencies with other Christians are forged through community living – leading to great personal growth while at college but often inability to cope alone within youth ministry posts.

The level of theological unity found at Cliff is rarely experienced outside of similar Christian communities, which potentially leads to relational difficulties when graduates entering church employment are faced with those of other theological persuasion and opinion.

Community life at Cliff is relevant in both its successes and failings in relation to preparing students for youth ministry. An ability to model authentic community, as experienced at Cliff, can offer immense potential in ministering to young people who themselves are largely community focussed. Lessons learnt in community can be beneficial when working alongside others and can be inspirational for future community-centred mission. Conversely, the stark distinctions between a supportive, wholly Christian environment and life 'outside the Cliff College greenhouse'[19] are for many difficult to readjust to. Unhelpful feelings of aloneness and reminiscence are often more prevalent for graduates than positive initiative in building inspiration and vision for community.

---

[18] Clarke D, *Breaking the Mould of Christendom* (Peterborough: Epworth, 2005), p.16.
[19] Clarke, *Director of Evangelism's Report* (March 2000)

Chapter Four

Full-time Church-based Youth Ministry

nalysis of youth worker job descriptions[1] revealed five main areas of responsibility:

1. Evangelism
2. Discipleship
3. Pastoral Care
4. Personal and Social Development
5. Involvement and Leadership of other Ministries within the Church

For holistic youth ministry, these should be equally important. Leadership, organisational and relational skills are required for each and are often crucial to the successes or failings of work carried out.

Evangelism
Recognition of culture and context is significant in evangelistic effectiveness, seeking to revitalise culture from within rather than oppress it from without.[2] 'It is essential that Christian youth workers

---

[1] Sample Job Descriptions, Appendix E, pp.129-135.
[2] Shorter A, *Toward a Theology of Inculturation* (Maryknoll, New York: Orbis Books, 1988), p.27.

take on board the challenge of finding appropriate ways to share the Gospel with young people.'[3]

Newbigin signals the importance of making the Gospel 'at home within a culture.'[4] An example of this is incultured evangelism within skateboarding cultures, where Christians have built skate parks, organised competitions and established magazines.[5] 'This niche ministry has given young people with little formal contact with the Church an opportunity to explore matters of faith and belief.'[6] While it would be inappropriate for every youth worker to replicate this example, the notion of inculturating the Gospel message is essential.

Within the context of inculturation, Newbigin's description of the Gospel 'making sense'[7] can appear misleading. Elements of Christ's teaching do not make worldly sense; loving those who hate you; blessing those who curse you; if someone strikes you on one cheek offering the other (Matt. 5:39–44 paraphrase) may appear to contradict a 'normal' response. Inculturation can make sense of Gospel themes such as love, trust, human existence and purpose. These values are of the utmost importance for evangelism amongst young people.

Discipleship
Evangelism that leads to conversion but fails to engage in discipleship falls short of Christ's commission to the Church (Matt. 28:19). If evangelism should take an encultured approach, so too should discipleship. Churches have been guilty of relying on structured courses for discipleship, potentially alienating young people from their culture, using teaching that may bear little relevance to their way of life. The aim of discipleship is to enable young people to explore the Christian faith for themselves, remembering that it is the Spirit of God who will lead them into truth.[8] *Gospel Exploded*[9] tells the story of encultured discipleship amongst young people in Bermondsey, London. 'The young people were like a tribe with their own language and customs, and our job was to root our teaching of Jesus in ideas they understood.'[10] Ward cautions that the ambiguity of free exploration

[3] Ward, *Youthwork,* p.59.
[4] Bosch D, *Transforming Mission: Paradigm Shifts in Theology and Mission* (Maryknoll, New York: Orbis Books, 1991), p.455.
[5] Brierley D, *Joined Up,* p.182.
[6] Brierley D, *Joined Up,* p.182.
[7] Newbigin L, *The Gospel in a Pluralist Society* (London: SPCK, 1997), p.141
[8] Ward, *Youthwork,* p.64.
[9] Mayo B, *Gospel Exploded* (London: Triangle, 1996)
[10] Mayo, *Gospel Exploded,* p.42.

'needs to be balanced with some idea of the limits of Christian expression and interpretation.'[11] There must be careful guarding against syncretism to maintain Gospel authenticity.

Discipleship in youth ministry should be incarnational, given integrity through personal example. This approach is seen in the ministry of Christ with the disciples throughout the gospels. Young people not only need to *hear* about authentic discipleship, they also need to *see* it modelled by those leading them in the faith.

Pastoral Care

The adage that young people do not care how much you know, until they know how much you care is simplistic, but remains true. Many young people desire genuine love and care, often not experienced in their homes. Listening is one of the key skills in youth ministry and forms the basis of pastoral care. Trust must be established between the young person and the youth worker, which can take time. Jesus invested time in people (e.g. John 4:1-26 where Jesus talked with a Samaritan woman). He listened, questioned, and showed true compassion. He gave words of instruction to the woman caught in adultery, saying, 'Go, and leave your life of sin' (John 8:11). Pastoral care with young people should balance words of comfort with words of wisdom. Additionally, issues of confidentiality and safeguarding are of paramount importance.

From a position of long-term pastoral care, spiritual and personal growth often occurs in a young person. Brierley's Relationship Triangle (overleaf)[12] shows the progression with young people from 'initial connection to positive relationship, pastoral support and ultimately lasting change.'[13] As the Relationship Triangle becomes narrower, the focus shifts from quantity of connection to quality of change.

Personal and Social Development of Young People

A significant element of youth ministry involves aiding young people's personal and social development alongside their spiritual development. This can include recreational activities, teaching and the delegation of responsibility amongst young people.

When developing a balanced programme for young people, youth workers need to consider holistically the areas within their job

---

[11] Ward, *Youthwork,* p.65.
[12] Brierley D, *What Every Volunteer Youth Worker Should Know,* (Carlisle: Spring Harvest Publishing Division and Authentic Lifestyle, 2003), p.57.
[13] Brierley D, *What Every Volunteer,* p.57.

descriptions as integrated, rather than distinct and detached. Young people must understand Christianity as a 'whole of life experience', where 'social' engages with 'spiritual'. A trait of postmodern society, witnessed in young people's lives, is the notion of a compartmentalised lifestyle. This is unhelpful to discipleship and spiritual growth; youth workers must emphasise faith as a lifestyle, rather than independent activity.

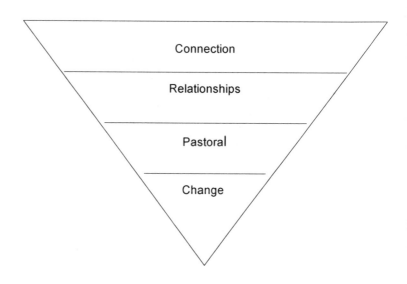

Figure 1: Brierley's Relationship Triangle[14]

Involvement and Leadership within the Church
Church-based youth ministry also involves active participation, and often leadership, in other areas of ministry. Youth workers may view this with disdain as it may detract from their main purpose and responsibility. In cases where task requirements within a job description are vague, blurred and misunderstood this may be true. One youth worker was expected to, 'write, put together and photocopy the weekly church notice sheet because there was no one else to do it.'[15] This is not helpful as it leads to time and effort spent on activities irrelevant to work with young people, sometimes to the detriment of

---

[14] Brierley D, *What Every Volunteer*, p.57.
[15] Graduate Interview 7, Appendix C, p.114.

youth ministry. Aspects of generic ministry that have direct correlation to work with young people are imperative for the youth worker. This includes building relationships with church members, those in church leadership and young people's families. One interviewee stated, 'Young people are unfortunately just a small part of being a youth worker. A much bigger part is taken up with interacting with the wider church and its leadership.'[16]

Youth ministry requires participation in the whole of church life. The employment of youth workers is often due to financial support of church members, who also offer essential prayer support. Youth workers must acknowledge these facts and seek to properly engage with the church. One interviewee admitted to, 'alienating a number of adults within the church'[17] as he felt he should, 'only really be working with the young people.'[18] This led to church members, 'losing confidence'[19] in his ability to do the job and eventually he resigned.

---

[16] Graduate Interview 2, Appendix C, p.95.
[17] Graduate Interview 7, Appendix C, p.115.
[18] Graduate Interview 7, Appendix C, p.115.
[19] Graduate Interview 7, Appendix C, p.115.

Chapter Five

Research Results
and Analysis

Database Research and Personal Knowledge

Between 1996-2005, there were 209 graduates who remained in the United Kingdom. The Cliff College Fellowship database, and personal knowledge of graduates, revealed the results below.

**Figure 2: Vocational Paths taken by Cliff Graduates
1996-2005**

Full-time, church-based youth ministry	Ministerial training	Church lay work	Para-church organisation
40	**22**	**18**	**11**
Further training / education	Secular employment	Other	Unknown
12	**21**	**11**	**74**

These results show that 19% of graduates entered youth ministry.

Questionnaires

Questionnaire 1 was distributed to the 74 graduates whose vocation was 'unknown', 74% of which were returned, revealing the following results:

Figure 3: Questionnaire 1 Results

Full-time, church-based youth ministry	Ministerial training	Church lay work	Para-church organisation
0	3	12	2
Further training / education	Secular employment	Other	Unreturned
7	18	13	19

These results revealed a clearer, though not definitive, account of graduates' vocational paths within the research timeframe.

Figure 4: Absolute Research Findings in Relation to Graduate Employment

Full-time, church-based youth ministry	Ministerial training	Church lay work	Para-church organisation
40	25	30	13
Further training / education	Secular employment	Other	Unknown
19	39	24	19

These results are to give context to the primary research concerning graduates who entered youth ministry. No further analysis has been carried out.

Questionnaire 2 was distributed to the 40 graduates known to have entered youth ministry posts, 75% of which were returned, revealing the following results. These have been examined and analysed in relation to Cliff's preparatory contribution to graduates' effectiveness in youth ministry.

73% of respondents were less than 26 years old when entering youth ministry. Within Higher Education, a large proportion of graduates generally fall between the ages of 21 and 25. In that respect, Cliff is no different. Previous research statistics show that approximately 67% of church-based youth workers are under 40;[1] this is evident in these results. It is perhaps therefore surprising that the 26–35 years group is only represented by 26%. Further research would be required to explicate this.

Postmodern society actively encourages younger people in leadership roles. However, inexperience and, at times, immaturity are sometimes synonymous with the younger generation. This is not always so, and should not be understood as a sweeping statement. Many respondents cited that their age and inexperience were influential in them failing to reach their potential as youth workers.[2] One respondent stated, 'I know if I was in a similar position now, I would definitely have done things differently and acted more responsibly.'[3] This naivety is perhaps most common in relational elements of youth ministry; 'Youth workers who are still quite young themselves are often very good at relating to the young people they are working with, but not so good at relating to adults, and this often results in problems which can escalate.'[4]

There are both advantages and disadvantages in employing younger people as youth workers, though each individual will possess strengths and weaknesses regardless of their age. As Nash suggests, youth workers aged 19–25 often relate more naturally to young people. They may have a better grasp of youth culture – similar tastes in music, recreation and media etc – and be able to more effectively inculturate the Gospel. Conversely, younger youth workers may lack tolerance with older, more traditional church members, appear impetuous, often desiring rapid change and misinterpret advice as criticism. One church leader stated:

---

[1] Gelder & Escott, *Profile of Youth Workers*, pp.4-5.
[2] Focus Group Extracts, Appendix A, pp.70-70; Questionnaire Results, Appendix B, pp.75-81; Graduate Interview 6, Appendix C, p.112.
[3] Graduate Interview 3, Appendix C, p.99.
[4] Sally Nash Interview, Appendix C, p.123.

One of the first things that the youth worker did when he started the job was to close down a new youth group that had been established for un-churched youngsters. I should have realised that that was a warning sign, because that happened without any proper consultation with me, I just discovered afterwards that a decision had been made.[5]

Youth workers who are over 25 have often been previously employed and may bring an increased level of maturity and responsibility to their work, often being better managers of time, people and work schedules. Notwithstanding these distinctions, it is imperative that broad judgements are not made in relation to age; perhaps a more significant factor is that, for a large proportion, their first youth ministry post was also their first experience of full-time employment.

Youth workers who have had full-time employment experience prior to studying at Cliff are arguably better equipped than those who have not. A first full-time job, in any field, invariably involves steep learning curves, grasping both employer and employee expectations. As 63% of youth workers within this research had never worked full-time, it is possible that many of their problems may have been linked to a lack of employment experience. Often, they 'simply don't know some of the basic elements of doing a full-time job...this can contribute to poor working relationships and escalate into much larger problems.'[6] Highlighting this, one church leader stated:

The youth worker was doing very little real work...he was there for the up-front stuff sometimes, but when it came down to the daily graft, and the consistent being there and working with people, that wasn't happening.[7]

While some churches may argue that their youth worker did less work than expected, Nash notes, 'it sometimes works the other way as well, and we find that some youth workers are doing too much, risking burnout.'[8] Working to excess often comes from a desire to please and succeed, particularly early in the post. Clear aims and objectives for the youth worker from line management, alongside

---

[5] Church Leader 1 Interview, Appendix C, p.85.
[6] Sally Nash Interview, Appendix C, p.123.
[7] Church Leader 1 Interview, Appendix C, p.83.
[8] Sally Nash Interview, Appendix C, p.123.

noticing early indications of overwork, are needed to prevent potential burnout. While students must be encouraged to be 'autonomous learners, taking responsibility for themselves,'[9] those involved in youth worker training perhaps, 'need to be more pro-active in making some things clear about what is expected as an employee.'[10]

Figure 5: Respondents Previous Youth Ministry Experience

Cliff Mission	Cliff Events	Voluntary church-based youth ministry	Voluntary statutory youth work	Para-church / Mission organisations	None / Minimal
24	13	18	1	5	4

These results show that the majority of respondents' previous youth ministry experience came through Cliff missions or events and voluntary youth ministry. This is concerning, as during the timeframe of this research, few missions were specifically focussed on youth ministry, so this experience would have been short-term and fleeting – and for a number of graduates this was their only prior experience. Similarly, the young age profile of graduates suggests a lack of long-term voluntary experience. Such experience is arguably insufficient as a preparatory means of equipping for youth ministry.

**Figure 6: Length of time Respondents were employed
in their initial Youth Ministry Post**
(Figures in brackets indicate those still employed in that position)

Less than 1 year	1 – 2 years	2 – 3 years	More than 3 years
4 (1)	11 (1)	6	9 (5)

---

[9] Sally Nash Interview, Appendix C, p.123.
[10] Sally Nash Interview, Appendix C, p.123.

At the time of researching, 23% of the thirty participants were still employed in their initial post. 80% of those who remained in their initial post for over three years stated on their questionnaire that they felt called to youth ministry, rather than it just being a job. A calling to youth ministry should not preclude moving jobs within such work, but this emphasises these respondents' commitment and understanding of the need for longevity in successful youth ministry.

57% of those who changed jobs worked in their initial post for no more than two years and 13% of these left within the first year of employment. This is a concerning statistic, which will have had implications for the churches, young people and youth workers involved. Consideration of each individual questionnaire has shown that only two of those leaving at or before the two year marker did so because their contract expired – indicating that at least 48% of respondents did not complete the three years indicated on their initial contract. A total of 73% of respondents indicated that their initial contract was for three years employment.

Figure 7: Reasons for Youth Workers Leaving their Initial Post

Moved to youth ministry post	Commenced ministerial training	Full-time youth ministry training	Other form of church-based work	Other – leaving church work
3	2	1	4	13

43% stayed in Christian ministry (in a variety of forms). It is possible to assume that these respondents had a positive experience of working for the church in their initial post, leading to their willingness to remain in church-based employment. They may have been called into other ministries, or chose to move away from youth ministry. Only 17% of those who changed jobs stayed within youth ministry, which possibly shows a defection of 83% - although all of these may not have permanently left youth ministry. This figure raises the question of whether many entering full-time youth ministry perceive it as a temporary employment option, rather than a vocational calling.

Youth workers and employers need to recognise the importance of longevity in effective youth ministry. It is common to desire immediate or swift results, without which many youth workers feel disillusioned, disappointed and often decide to leave their employment. One interviewee in emphasising the need for perseverance stated, 'The most fruitful years of my ministry have been after four years in the same job.'[11]

Churches that have invested time, energy and finance into employing a youth worker are inevitably disappointed when the employment is curtailed. Obviously, in some cases, there is a mismatch of post and employee. When this is realised early in the appointment, it is arguably better for the contract to be ended as swiftly and as amicably as possible. Notwithstanding this, it is invariably a painful experience. One of the church leaders interviewed stated the youth worker, 'left after five weeks, leaving the churches in a mess'[12] as far as the work with young people was concerned. The young people will be affected by the youth worker leaving and may wonder if they have been responsible in some way.

54% of those leaving who cited 'other' reasons for doing so mentioned stress, unhappiness and disagreement rather than a change in their personal circumstances or contractual end of employment. The repercussions for youth workers who have a negative employment experience are numerous. Many of these youth workers are relatively young, often with no previous employment experience. Resigning due to stress related illness at such a young age cannot be helpful for them in relation to future employment. Moreover, issues such as loss of confidence, crises of faith, and feelings of failure are amongst personal struggles associated with such curtailment. 23% who changed jobs outside of church work offered no further explanation for this choice.

A total of 37% of respondents remain employed in youth ministry. This figure seems more positive than the above results. However those remaining in their original posts have yet to change jobs, and their choices at that point remain to be seen. 57% are still involved in church-based ministry. However, a total of 43% are no longer involved in church-based ministry. It is dangerous to imply that non church-based work is not 'ministry' and to assume that, because the church no longer employs respondents, they are not involved in ministry. Calling to church-based work is not always permanent or long-term; but notwithstanding these statements, the figures of those leaving church employment remain relatively high, causing some concern.

---

[11] Graduate Interview 5, Appendix C, p.106.
[12] Church Leader 1 Interview, Appendix C, p.86.

42

58% of respondents had not been offered further training specifically in youth ministry. As none had any previous youth ministry training besides the little they received at Cliff, it seems clear that youth specific training would have been beneficial. This would have highlighted and addressed training needs, and may have helped to prevent certain mistakes from being made. 63% felt there were insufficient support structures in place for them as employees, in relation to ether management or personal support.[13] This is explored more thoroughly later.

Figure 8: Number of Years Respondents Studied
at Cliff College
(Figures in brackets indicate actual respondent numbers)

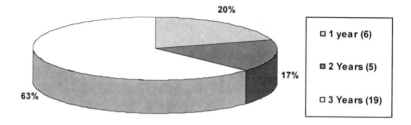

The length of time graduates studied at Cliff appeared to have little bearing on their success. Two of the respondents who had stayed in the same job since graduating had completed only two years' study. This potentially negates the notion that the longer a student has studied, the greater their potential success in employment will be, due to greater knowledge and experience. Additional factors influencing success in youth ministry are discussed further later.

Respondents were generally positive concerning their experiences whilst at Cliff. The graph shows few rated any of their training at Cliff as poor, with the average respondent rating almost all aspects as very good. Many viewed the spiritual and theological dimensions of the course as excellent, though no other areas gained such high rating. It is apparent that graduates on the whole view Cliff positively and, from the spiritual and educational perspectives, Cliff excels.

---

[13] Questionnaire 2 Results, Appendix B, p.79.

Figure 9: Respondents' Ratings of Cliff College as Preparation for Youth Ministry

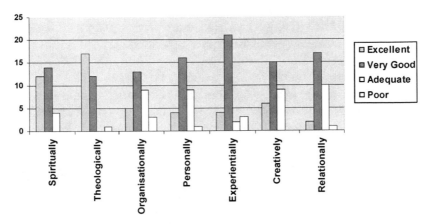

Whilst these results are positive, further investigation into responses was required in order to ascertain the reasons why graduates responded as they did. This was achieved through one to one interviews, which provided a much fuller picture, in some cases contradictory to the questionnaire results. This shows the importance of qualitative research for such a study as this. When people have the opportunity to consider their responses within a conversation, they are able to properly assess their views and feelings.

Interviews

The interviews conducted have been analysed in relation to the outlined elements of the Cliff Experience and the youth ministry sample job descriptions. Three main areas were covered:

i. Analysis of Full-Time Undergraduate Study at Bible College as Preparation for Youth Ministry

Cliff College, while offering a BA in Theology, cannot offer a significant amount of training for students focussed specifically upon youth ministry, although it may offer better ministry preparation in other areas. Nash suggests that, 'What Bible colleges do, that perhaps youth specific training institutions aren't able to do, is to root their training in spiritual and ministerial formation.'[14] Many youth specific training institutions receive government grants for the professional training of youth workers, resulting in Joint Negotiating Committee (JNC) qualifications. This dramatically affects the way courses are

---

[14] Sally Nash Interview, Appendix C, p.123.

delivered to comply with Government legislation mandates. Bible colleges, though still in compliance with relevant validating partners, have significantly more freedom. The dimensions of the previously outlined Cliff College Experience are further examined here in relation to their effect on youth ministry preparation.

a. Academic Study

Whilst Higher Education does not necessarily equate to success as a youth worker, it can contribute in providing tools for further learning, which is essential for Christian discipleship. The majority of interviewees maintained that Cliff is, 'really good as an academic institution.'[15] Many claim to have 'learnt a lot about theology, the Bible and evangelism,'[16] gaining insight into mission, culture, church, leadership and so on. In relation to preparation for youth ministry, one interviewee noted that his training had helped him to understand how people think differently, and have differing views and beliefs.[17] This appreciation of Cliff's academic excellence should be highlighted. Cliff's commitment to the outworking of theological study within mission and evangelism means that students are not only academically stimulated, but learn how to apply this theology. As one interviewee stated, 'I went to Cliff wanting to learn what authentic, effective evangelism really meant, and how that could take effect for me as a witness to Christ's work in my life.'[18]

b. Practical Experience

Many churches are not as contemporary in their thinking and practice of mission and evangelism as Cliff graduates may be.[19] Youth workers must be able to work with people as they are, not forcing immediate change or appearing 'judgemental and arrogant in their approach,'[20] but patiently building mutual trust and acceptance. Much more can be achieved by this approach.

Working for a church bears some similarity to Cliff missions in terms of activities; however there are many differences. One such distinction is within relational aspects of ministry. Cliff missions are mostly short-term and relationships are often established but rarely developed. Cliff students do not fully experience relational issues in

---

[15] Graduate Interview 1, Appendix C, p.92.
[16] Graduate Interview 1, Appendix C, p.92.
[17] Graduate Interview 5, Appendix C, p.106.
[18] Graduate Interview 7, Appendix C, p.115.
[19] Graduate Interview 3, Appendix C, p.97.
[20] Church Leader 2 Interview, Appendix C, p.88.

churches, some of which involve conflict situations. When graduates enter youth ministry, such relational elements are new experiences and are often not handled appropriately. The ability to function relationally is vital in church ministry; poor relationships frequently lead to youth workers becoming disillusioned. Their employment position breaking down, sometimes beyond repair, may follow. Many interviewees noted this. It was highlighted by one, who stated:

> If someone in the church where we were on mission was annoying or irritating, we knew that in a few days time, we'd be on our way back to Cliff. This didn't teach us about working through tricky situations, and treading carefully with what we said, because if it did all go pear shaped, we weren't going to have to face those people again. Full-time church-based youth ministry is not like that. If I mess up, I do have to face that person again.[21]

Much of Cliff's practical experience is in the context of team missions. Teamwork is an appropriate approach to contemporary ministry and so Cliff's emphasis could be seen as productive and helpful. However, Cliff teams operate quite differently from team ministries in churches. Students are mixed in terms of age, ability, experience and personality but there is often a close bond between members of Cliff mission teams – and members can become too reliant upon each other. Interviewees maintained that working within teams on Cliff missions provided some excellent experiences but ministry is, 'just the opposite when you leave and go to work for a church. It can feel incredibly isolated.'[22]

This disparity between missions and ministry is in part being addressed through the increase in students engaging in individual placements. Clarke, an advocate of the placement approach, stressed:

> There needs to be a greater emphasis on placements within the college programme, and less on missions, so that students leave college and enter church-based ministry situations with a more realistic idea, and are willing to accept the situation as it is, and not as they would want it to be.[23]

---

[21] Graduate Interview 1, Appendix C, p.93.

[22] Graduate Interview 6, Appendix C, p.111.

[23] Church Leader 1 Interview, Appendix C, p.85.

For practical experience to have validity in equipping graduates for youth ministry, it is essential that students receive relevant practical experience. One interviewee commenting on his mission experience over three years at Cliff stated that, 'only a fraction was concerned with youth work.'[24]

Graduates cannot know if full-time youth ministry is for them unless they are exposed to and involved in substantial amounts of ministry with young people. This highlights a point raised earlier concerning the lack of experience graduates had when entering youth ministry. One stated, 'I had no idea what I wanted to do when I left Cliff, but I thought it would be something I would be good at and enjoy doing.'[25] This level of naivety would rarely be possible in other careers or vocations, so why should it be acceptable within youth ministry? I suggest it should not; students should gain essential knowledge and experience, preferably within ongoing, local placements.

c. Tutorial Contact

As previously outlined in Chapter Three, students have substantial tutorial support throughout their time at Cliff. At Levels One and Two, tutorials predominantly focus upon tasks that students complete, assessment guidance and personal pastoral journals. Tutorial contact concerning vocational discernment generally happens at Level Three; students explore what it means to be called by God, then more personal aspects of call are considered individually, 'Where their gifts, abilities, motives, and so on are discussed in some depth.'[26] Firth indicates, 'The problem with doing these sessions so late in the course is that by this time most of them have already worked out what they want to do when they leave Cliff.'[27]

'Must a youth worker be called by God or must they simply be willing to do the job?'[28] This is a fundamental question that must be addressed in the analysis of youth workers' success. The concept of vocation within the Christian tradition is rooted in Biblical material pertaining to call. In her research into vocation amongst youth workers, Sam Richards highlights some important points. Many participants in

---

[24] Graduate Interview 4, Appendix C, p.101.
[25] Graduate Interview 6, Appendix C, p.109.
[26] David Firth Interview, Appendix C, p.121.
[27] David Firth Interview, Appendix C, p.121.
[28] Graduate Interview 4, Appendix C, p.103.

her study, 'saw themselves fundamentally as working for God,'[29] taking the 'vocational stance that it is more than a job.'[30] Many viewed 'youth work as ministry, but felt this was not understood or recognised by others,'[31] perhaps due to the significantly less intense process of discernment for a person considering youth ministry, than for other ordained positions in the church. Many view such positions as associated less with 'calling' than ordained positions of ministry. This may be partially responsible for apparently skewed perceptions of youth work highlighted by Richards' research.

Interviewees in this study emphasised the importance of 'responding to God's call'[32] as a motive for youth ministry. One stated, 'I always had a sense that I was serving the Lord first, and in a way the Church second.'[33] Some interviewees acknowledged that they and others known to them were, 'just not suited or called to youth work.'[34] One noted that many seemed to think youth ministry an easy job they could do while they decided what they really wanted to do for a career.[35]

Most interviewees confirmed that Cliff could have taught more about 'calling', the addressing of issues such as knowing where and to whom God is calling and testing a call was cited as lacking within the course.[36] It is perhaps due to a lack of teaching that some graduates entered youth ministry.

One interviewee claimed an unspoken expectation that graduates either, 'do a PGCE, ministerial training, or some sort of church-based job – usually youth work or lay work.'[37] IIe felt that proper vocational guidance was lacking at Cliff,[38] thus many graduates enter youth ministry somewhat naively.

Since becoming Level Three course director, Firth has encouraged students to think carefully about vocational options. Unfortunately, many of those interviewed for this research cited this was not emphasised during their period of study. One noted, 'Cliff

---

[29] Richards S, *An Exploration of the Notion of 'Sense of Vocation' Among Christian Youth Workers* (University of Oxford: Unpublished PhD Thesis, 2005), p.161.
[30] Richards, *An Exploration of the Notion of 'Sense of Vocation'*, p.161.
[31] Richards, *An Exploration of the Notion of 'Sense of Vocation'*, p.161.
[32] Graduate Interview 4, Appendix C, p.100.
[33] Graduate Interview 5, Appendix C, p.105.
[34] Graduate Interview 4, Appendix C, p.103.
[35] Graduate Interview 5, Appendix C, p.107.
[36] Graduate Interview 5, Appendix C, p.107.
[37] Graduate Interview 2, Appendix C, p.94.
[38] Graduate Interview 2, Appendix C, p.95.

needs to offer some proper careers advice. If this had been available when I was there, I might not have ever applied for the job I did.'[39] Students should be aware of all their career options from Level One, which would help to broaden their vision concerning vocation.

d. Community Life

Interviews have revealed a suggestion that the longer a student studies at Cliff, the more institutionalised they become. Students leaving after one or two years may find leaving the community less distressing than those who have studied for three or more years. Interview comments included:

> Life at Cliff revolves very much around the Cliff community, and that can become like a bubble, very inward looking, very isolated from the outside world... To go from that extreme to working for a church in a wider community, working with people who have lives outside of church, who have other priorities and so on, and to generally find yourself in a situation that's very different from life at Cliff is a big deal...I wasn't prepared for that huge change.[40]

Whilst there are clear advantages to completing the degree course, from an academic and future career perspective, the evidence from this research appears to suggest the associated disadvantages of staying for a prolonged time within a close knit community such as Cliff College.

Cliff must recognise this dilemma; community life is encouraged whilst students are at Cliff and is welcomed by them. However, it is recognised throughout this research that the experience of leaving a loving and caring community left respondents feeling somewhat bereft when alone in a youth ministry post.

ii. Analysis of the Ongoing Practice of Youth Ministry in Relation to Graduates' Own Experiences

It can be argued that the true test of whether a graduate is sufficiently prepared for their first youth ministry appointment is evidenced within their actual achievements in the post. Interviewees' analysis of their own performance and comments from those training or with management responsibility for youth workers are valuable here. The

---

[39] Graduate Interview 3, Appendix C, p.99.
[40] Graduate Interview 1, Appendix C, p.92.

following areas of youth ministry practice have been examined in relation to their contribution to graduates' employment experiences.

a. Effectiveness within the Post

Effectiveness in ministry is difficult to assess and often depends on one's perspective. Success could be an increase in young people's church attendance or in giving one young person a sense of worth and purpose for their life. Is failure something to be ashamed of or embraced, within the context of learning? I suggest that, within youth ministry, the terms 'success' and 'failure' should not be used in stark contrast, though this should not preclude an analysis of effectiveness.

It is normal to judge our own performances either more or less favourably than others would. Some youth workers, from a desire to impress, will analyse their work by accentuating what they see as positive and minimising the negative. Others may fail to appreciate positive outcomes, thus presenting a more sombre account of their achievements.

Effectiveness, in some churches, is measured by comparison to previous youth workers. This is unhelpful for the current employee, particularly in the early stages of their employment. One interviewee stated, 'The problem was that some people were always comparing me to the other youth workers...that was quite hard.'[41] This led to the youth worker experiencing feelings of inadequacy just weeks into the appointment.

Inexperience can cause youth workers to try and replicate successful styles of youth work they have observed. This was raised by one church leader; the youth worker, who had 'previous experience with a very large, progressively thinking church elsewhere,'[42] felt that 'model of youth work was the best way forward,'[43] and attempted a similar model within the church where he was employed. However the church leader indicated, 'that's simply not where we are here.'[44] A model of ministry that is successful in one context may not necessarily be successful in another. Appreciating the local situation is vital.

It is important for youth workers to be self-aware and secure in themselves. Where these are lacking, youth workers may appear defensive, at times dismissing offers of assistance and support. Effective youth ministry must be collaborative and not autonomous. The management and integration of volunteers is essential, which can

---

[41] Graduate Interview 7, Appendix C, p.113.
[42] Church Leader 1 Interview, Appendix C, p.85.
[43] Church Leader 1 Interview, Appendix C, p.85.
[44] Church Leader 1 Interview, Appendix C, p.85.

only be achieved successfully when the importance of egalitarian leadership is recognised without neglecting their authority as an employee. One church leader, speaking of an effective youth worker he had employed, stated, 'He enabled others to be involved. People that you'd never have believed would do youth work, got involved in things and found out that they actually enjoyed it.'[45] One interviewee, employed as a Circuit youth worker whose role involved equipping, supporting and the general management of a large number of volunteers, stated he had 'no idea really how to deal with volunteer staff'.[46] Teaching on facilitating good volunteer structures within the ongoing practice of youth ministry perhaps needs to be included in Cliff's 'Evangelism and Young People' module.

b. Management and Support Structures
Youth workers in their first post and particularly their first full-time job need comprehensive levels of employer support. Although management and support are often linked, there are some clear distinctions. Management concerns the implementing of work schedules and contractual agreement adherences. Support, though it may incorporate some of these aspects, is more concerned with the holistic, mental, physical and spiritual welfare of the youth worker. Many youth workers experience problems when their management and support structures merge, often with management issues overshadowing support structures. Nash considers this distinction important, noting that pastoral support is best facilitated outside of management structures. 'This can bring tensions for clergy whose primary motivation is pastoral, and who see the youth worker as someone they have spiritual responsibility for.'[47] However, boundaries can often become blurred and pastoral confidentialities can be used in a context more pertinent to a management issue.[48]

One interviewee noted, 'My line management structure does not always work that well, as everyone thinks that they should have their say in what I do and how I do it.'[49] This will inevitably cause frustration and confusion. Line management has been defined as, 'the continuous process by which the manager directs, supports, motivates, protects, checks the work, provides opportunities for systematic review,

---

[45] Church Leader 2 Interview, Appendix C, p.88.

[46] Graduate Interview 4, Appendix C, p.102.

[47] Nash S, *Supervising Youth Workers* (Cambridge: Grove Books Limited, 2006), p.20.

[48] Nash, *Supervising Youth Workers,* p.20.

[49] Graduate Interview 4, Appendix C, p.101.

consults and passes information to and from the worker.'[50] In this there must be balance between the needs of the organisation, the needs of the worker and the relationship between the worker and management. If these are unstable problems can arise.

This research indicates that it is relationship breakdown that causes problems within line management. In questionnaire and interview responses, issues of relational tension between youth workers and line managers were raised, a common sentiment though expressed in different ways by participants in the study.[51] In some cases, this may have been due to a 'personality clash'[52] between the youth worker and their line manager.

Whilst there are no straightforward answers to this problem, prevention is usually better than a cure. Cliff should emphasise the maintenance of healthy, working relationships. This should include teaching on handling conflict, responding to authority, and creating effective management structures for those who may enter jobs lacking in such structuring.

A comparison can be drawn between youth workers in their first post and probationary ministers. The first year of any new vocation necessitates learning and transition. For the probationer, this initial phase of ministry takes place within a formal structure and with the provision of ongoing support and guidance. In contrast, many youth workers feel unsupported, unclear of what is expected of them and many gradually, or in some cases rapidly become disillusioned. Young people are as important as adults and lay work is apparently perceived to be as important as ordained ministry,[53] so why should there be disparity of support within the first year of work between these positions within the continuum of full-time ministry? Greater emphasis should be placed on appropriate support for full-time church-based youth workers, akin to that provided for probationary ministers.

It is important that although many interviewees cited problems with management and support structures, some emphasised the positive experiences, particularly Interviewee 5, stating:

---

[50] Ingram G and Harris J, *Delivering Good Youth Work* (Lyme Regis: Russell House, 2001), pp.105-107.

[51] Questionnaire 2 Results, Appendix B, pp.77-81; Graduate Interview Transcripts, Appendix C, pp.90-116; Church Leader 1 Interview, Appendix C, pp.82-86.

[52] Questionnaire 2 Results, Appendix B, p.79.

[53] Lay work forms part of the continuum of vocational discernment, alongside ordained ministries within the Methodist Church Foundation Training course

I felt supported by different people in different ways…I always felt the minister was supportive. There were times when we may not have understood each other, but he encouraged me in his own way and gave good advice…The church leaders were always very positive and would spur me on.[54]

This interviewee has been in youth ministry since graduating in 1998 and shows perhaps the most maturity of all interviewees, particularly concerning management and support. This is evident from comments such as, 'Support is a two way street, you have to play your part in the process, and not just sit there doing nothing, then complain when you don't feel supported,'[55] and, 'Whilst I always felt supported, the job wasn't always plain sailing. You have to learn to take the rough with the smooth, and work through tough times, not just give up at the first hurdle.'[56]

c. Employment Expectations

Within any employment, there are expectations on the employer and on the employee. Questionnaire 2 results revealed that 63% of graduates had never had a full-time job before their employment as a youth worker,[57] thus various aspects of employment were unknown to them. From basic expectations such as the fulfilment of contractual agreements concerning working hours, time off and general adherence to line management structures by the employee; to more complex issues of employment law concerning their rights as an employee. As one interviewee expressed, 'There needs to be more information on what to expect when you start a youth work job with a church. It's very different from voluntary youth work or Cliff missions.'[58]

This research has indicated that graduates do not have clear expectations of what is required upon entering full-time youth ministry. This was expressed by one interviewee:

Cliff was a great place and I learnt a lot about the Bible and theology, but in some ways, that wasn't all I needed to know when I started my job as a youth worker… it

---

[54] Graduate Interview 5, Appendix C, p.105.
[55] Graduate Interview 5, Appendix C, p.105.
[56] Graduate Interview 5, Appendix C, p.106.
[57] Questionnaire 2 Results, Appendix B, p.77.
[58] Graduate Interview 7, Appendix C, p.116.

felt a bit like I was in at the deep end, and had to either sink or swim.[59]

'Many churches have high expectations concerning youth workers, disproportionate to the expectations they have concerning other ministries in the life of the church.'[60] The pressure of unrealistic expectations is common amongst youth workers. One interviewee felt coerced to work over and above his contractual agreement. This was partly due to the minister working long hours, rarely taking time off and apparently expecting the same level of commitment from the youth worker.[61] Whilst youth ministry should ideally be seen as 'more than a job,'[62] and does involve unsociable hours, such high expectations in a youth worker's first post may result in the collapse of the appointment and cynicism towards church-based work.

Many youth workers give the impression that youth ministry is easy. This is a huge misconception; it is highly probable that where youth ministry is perceived as an easy option most employment problems occur. An example of this misunderstanding can be seen in a comment made by one interviewee, 'A youth worker has to find 40 hours work to do per week. What can you actually do for that amount of time every week when young people are at school?'[63] The idea that a youth worker would be short of work while young people attended school is concerning as it shows a failure to grasp the notion of strategic planning and careful preparation. Steve Tilley researched common complaints expressed by clergy about their youth workers who stated, 'They do not get up early enough in the morning, they are very untidy and poor at administration. No one knows where they are and they spend all their time playing on the computer.'[64] Whilst these may appear harsh and are not true of all youth workers, in cases where these perceptions are true, it is likely that the behaviour of such youth workers will cause negative experiences for all involved.

Many youth workers fall short of employer expectation, often through lack of work due largely to unavoidable ignorance. Cliff can prepare graduates better for employment generally in this area. Theological, ethical and practical teaching on the subject of work and

---

[59] Graduate Interview 7, Appendix C, p.115.

[60] Sally Nash Interview, Appendix C, p.123.

[61] Graduate Interview 2, Appendix C, p.95.

[62] Richards, An Exploration of the Notion of 'Sense of Vocation', p.161.

[63] Graduate Interview 3, Appendix C, p.99.

[64] Nash, Supervising Youth Workers, p.6. (I have been unable to locate Tilley's original research from which Nash quotes.)

employment would improve knowledge and understanding of what should and should not be expected of them by an employer.

Failure to acknowledge struggles and difficulties is another root cause of many youth workers' difficulties, not least those in their first post. Fear of showing weakness and ignorance, desiring to please, determination to succeed and having no one to trust to talk about problems with[65] were noted in the Focus Group as to why youth workers did not acknowledge problems they were experiencing, particularly within the first six months of the job. Cliff should encourage students to acknowledge weakness, not as a negative trait or as failure, but as a positive discipline of personal and spiritual growth and development. A healthy understanding and recognition of personal awareness is essential for any ministry.

Churches, as employers, also face criticism, not only for their lack of support discussed previously, but also at times for ambiguous job descriptions. Dave Edwins, founder of On Track Ministries,[66] notes that some churches, 'don't know what they want'[67] from a youth worker. He continues, stating that there is often a, 'lack of clarity and vision.'[68] This was confirmed by many interviewees, commenting, 'the objectives weren't really thought through'[69] and, 'It was never really clear whether my role was to lead all the groups or just act as a resource. This grey area caused a lot of problems for me and the church because nothing was ever clear or defined.'[70]

One interviewee was devastated to be told by her employer, 'You weren't what we expected.'[71] Expectations from the church were, 'vague from the start,'[72] so it was difficult for the youth worker to know what the church expected. The youth worker understandably felt hurt and let down. She concluded, 'The job had made me suffer with stress in a way I had never experienced before, and has made me much more cautious about working for the Church ever again.'[73]

Edwins recognises that, 'churches have a responsibility to encourage, mentor and guide youth workers.'[74] Interviewees rarely

---

[65] Focus Group Extracts, Appendix A, pp.70-74.

[66] On Track is an independent organisation aimed at supporting graduates, usually from Moorlands College in Dorset.

[67] Dave Edwins Interview, Appendix C, p.117.

[68] Dave Edwins Interview, Appendix C, p.117.

[69] Graduate Interview 2, Appendix C, p.95.

[70] Graduate Interview 6, Appendix C, p.109.

[71] Graduate Interview 6, Appendix C, p.110.

[72] Graduate Interview 6, Appendix C, p.109.

[73] Graduate Interview 6, Appendix C, p.112.

[74] Dave Edwins Interview, Appendix C, p.117.

experienced this. Comments such as: 'I felt the staff to be unsupportive and I didn't feel that people wanted me there most of the time, or maybe it was just that they were too busy to care,'[75] and, 'I was left to fend for myself'[76] appear to indicate a lack of pastoral concern for this youth worker.

For youth workers who are often young, inexperienced in relation to employment and youth ministry, and straight out of the familiarity and security of Cliff College, there are certain things that churches must recognise. It is crucial that the aims and objectives are clear and that these are reasonable; that line management and support structures are well conceived and operate efficiently, addressing any points of concern with the youth worker's employment as they arise and that ministers view youth workers as working 'partners' rather than 'assistants', thus facilitating a sense of equality in ministry.

iii. Analysis of Graduates' Effectiveness in the Position including their Reflective Learning

Essential learning and evaluation can occur through reflection. Although youth workers can be reticent in acknowledging mistakes whilst in their posts, this research has facilitated helpful reflection for many. One commented that he had never 'really talked openly about these experiences to anyone'[77] and had found the interview to be 'healing.'[78] Graduates' own reflective analysis, examined here, will be helpful to them for future employment and ministry, alongside being useful to Cliff in preparing graduates.

a. Right Calling – Wrong Job

All youth ministry posts are not the same. Students considering youth ministry often make poor choices when deciding which posts to apply for. A large church, with a good, established youth ministry may seem more appealing, particularly if the salary is substantial. However, certain posts will be significantly more challenging than others. Graduates should be cautious about which they apply for and learn to assess the probable demands from job descriptions. Some posts are simply not appropriate as first time positions for graduates with little experience in youth ministry. As one interviewee commented, 'I

---

[75] Graduate Interview 6, Appendix C, p.110.
[76] Graduate Interview 6, Appendix C, p.110.
[77] Graduate Interview 7, Appendix C, p.116.
[78] Graduate Interview 7, Appendix C, p.116.

actually went for the wrong job. I wasn't ready for it at that time…it was just too big for me and I couldn't handle it.'[79]

Ideally, graduates who feel called to full-time, church-based youth ministry should consider posts that they are sure have been properly conceived. Also, they should not dismiss smaller, less demanding posts that perhaps come with smaller salaries. Such jobs are good for those in first time employment or with little experience in youth ministry. It is preferable for the graduate to excel in a post that is stretching, though attainable within their existing knowledge and experience, than to dramatically fail in a role far beyond their experience. Cliff must emphasise to students exploring the plethora of youth ministry advertisements, that whilst none should be seen as easy, some will undoubtedly be more appropriate for them than others.

This issue was discussed at length in the Focus Group and participants agreed that Cliff should positively emphasise the benefits of 'learning the trade'[80] of youth ministry in a post that is challenging, though not overwhelming. This would provide graduates with essential experience, facilitate the development of skills and prepare them sufficiently for a more demanding youth ministry post at a later date.

Numerous church youth ministry posts are advertised each week, to the extent that there may not be enough candidates for each post. Graduates may make mistakes in applying for posts beyond their experience and skills. Similarly, churches may be wooed by qualifications and appoint inexperienced candidates in order to fill their post.

Cliff graduates often present themselves and their achievements well on application forms and at interview. Both church leaders who were interviewed agreed that graduates showed good presentation skills.[81] One stated that the graduate, 'came across very well. He was confident, answered the questions thoughtfully and with reasonably good knowledge.'[82] This shows improvement in terms of Cliff's preparatory work with students for interviews. Clarke indicated that during his term as Director of Evangelism, church leaders had claimed that 'Cliff students did not present themselves well at interview, nor did they give very good CV's.'[83] Clearly some progress has been made,

---

[79] Graduate Interview 3, Appendix C, p.99.

[80] Focus Group Extracts, Appendix A, p.73.

[81] Church Leader 1 Interview, Appendix C, p.84; Church Leader 2 Interview, Appendix C, p.88.

[82] Church Leader 2 Interview, Appendix C, p.88.

[83] Church Leader 1 Interview, Appendix C, p.84.

though further investigation would be required to accurately validate this.

b. Wrong Calling – Wrong Job

Unfortunately, some graduates who enter youth ministry realise after they have started the work that this is not what they feel called to do. Responsibility and commitment, vision and leadership are required for the work, alongside passion for working with young people. Whilst these qualities are often present amongst volunteers, youth ministry employees should champion them, some of whom struggle to cope with the demands of the work. One interviewee stated, 'I would not have become a youth worker in the local church. I would have got a job and done youth work voluntarily.'[84] This interviewee clearly desired to work with young people, though with hindsight he would have preferred to be a volunteer. He acknowledged his desperation for a job when leaving Cliff, and a naïve belief that the job 'had to be in the Church.'[85] It is unfortunate that better careers guidance was not given to this graduate. Improved vocational guidance, as noted earlier, may help to prevent further graduates embarking on careers that are clearly not right for them. Sadly, this interviewee is no longer involved in youth ministry, moreover has become disillusioned with the Church following his negative experiences. He felt 'so hurt by church leaders'[86] he is 'still reluctant to go back to Church.'[87]

c. Reflective Learning

Interviewees were asked what they had learnt from their first youth ministry post and, in retrospect, what they might have done differently. One respondent commented, 'I could have listened to people more, who probably knew what they were doing far better than I did...I didn't want to admit that I wasn't totally sure what I was doing.'[88] Cliff needs to foster a mindset within students of authentic learning, particularly from those with greater experience. Some students should adopt a more humble approach, acknowledging their inexperience and desiring to learn more. This was strongly emphasised by the longest serving youth worker in this study. He maintains, 'Students should be encouraged to constantly learn from others who have been in ministry a long time.'[89]

---

[84] Graduate Interview 2, Appendix C, p.96.
[85] Graduate Interview 2, Appendix C, p.96.
[86] Graduate Interview 2, Appendix C, p.96.
[87] Graduate Interview 2, Appendix C, p.96.
[88] Graduate Interview 7, Appendix C, p.116.
[89] Graduate Interview 5, Appendix C, p.108.

He advocates that, rather than wanting to impress, they should admit 'that they don't know very much, and...learn from others. Being afraid to be vulnerable is a dangerous place to be, especially as a new youth worker.[90]

One interviewee recognised his compliance with an untenable job description as a circuit youth worker hindered the effectiveness of the work. He reflected, 'I would have developed the job into something workable much sooner. I continued to work at a job for three years which simply didn't work.'[91]This shows a lack of confidence in interacting with management groups in order to develop a more appropriate job description, and perhaps a fear of admitting inability to fulfil the original description.

Interviewees readily accepted that they had made mistakes in the area of relationships with church leaders and members, acknowledging similar struggles in managing volunteers as discussed earlier. These can quickly lead to increased pressure on young graduates, who already may feel somewhat 'out of their depth,'[92] resulting in further strain on working relationships.

While Cliff can improve teaching in this area, there are limitations on what can be learnt about relational work, managing volunteers and handling conflict situations in the lecture room. Arguably these skills are better learnt through practical experience. Short-term missions and placements provide some measure of experience concerning teamwork, leadership and the development of healthy, working relationships; though this research indicates that long-term experience may prove to be more beneficial.

---

[90] Graduate Interview 5, Appendix C, p.108.
[91] Graduate Interview 4, Appendix C, p.102.
[92] Dave Edwins Interview, Appendix C, p.117.

Chapter Six

Conclusions and Recommendations

This research has examined and evaluated full-time undergraduate study at Cliff College as a means of preparation for full-time church-based youth ministry. It is important to remember that Cliff is a Bible College, not specifically a youth ministry training college. Cliff can 'never prepare all students for all possible employment routes.'[1] This should not be considered to be pejorative, rather constructive in the continued theological, spiritual and personal equipping of ordinary Christians to be extraordinary ambassadors for Christ in the world.

This research shows that there are four main elements to succeeding in full-time, church-based youth ministry:

- Calling from God
- Sufficient Training
- Attitude and Spirituality of the Youth Worker
- Responsibility of the Church as the Employer

---

[1] Graduate Interview 5, Appendix C, p.108.

Clarke raised some of these elements during his term as Director of Evangelism, (1994–2002). Recognising issues facing church workers, many of who had left employment sooner than expected, he wrote a paper[2] outlining his concerns that have been analysed within this research. Clarke's preliminary research was insightful and signalled the problems addressed here.

Calling from God

A person should be called by God to be successful and content in full-time youth ministry. Participants in this study recognised the importance of calling and the distinctions between paid and voluntary youth ministry. Without a clear calling by God to this ministry, many become disillusioned and disheartened.

Sufficient Training

All careers require a level of training; a person cannot be expected to possess the specialist knowledge or skills required to effectively do a job without sufficient instruction. This research indicates that, whilst Cliff provides excellent theological and spiritual guidance, it cannot fully equip students for the specialised areas of ministry, not least full-time youth ministry. Graduates from Cliff seeking to enter youth ministry should view their undergraduate study as preparation for further youth-specific training. Alternatively, they should approach their first post as probationers, aiming to learn and develop their skills, ideally in conjunction with further formal training. This is how Cliff's part-time 'Diploma in Youth, Mission and Ministry' course is best experienced; by practitioners honing their abilities as full-time youth workers.

Attitude and Spirituality of the Youth Worker

These two are often intrinsically linked; our attitude to ministry can influence our spirituality and vice versa. This research suggests that church-based youth ministry involves working in partnership with lay and ordained. A youth worker must take seriously the call to resemble the attitude of Christ, 'having the same love, being one in spirit and purpose. Do[ing] nothing out of vain conceit, but in humility consider[ing] others better than yourselves' (Philippians 2:2–3). 'Developing a teachable spirit and character are vital to youth work.'[3] Similarly, sustaining spirituality is equally important. How can one

---

[2] Clarke P, *Why do Many Recent Former Cliff Students Leave Lay Worker Posts Early?* (Cliff College: 2000)
[3] Graduate Interview 5, Appendix C, p.108.

responsible for the discipleship of young people engage with this task authentically and effectively if their own spirituality is neglected? It is vital for youth workers to maintain spiritual discipline within their own lives, in order to effectively minister amongst young people.

Responsibility of the Church as the Employer

This research shows that unless the church as employer has sufficiently planned the post, problems may well arise for both the youth worker and the church. Ambiguous job descriptions, unrealistic expectations, lack of further training opportunities and poor management all contributed to the dissatisfaction of participants in this study with their employment, some to the point of resignation. For others, whilst these factors may not have been the primary reason for their problems in the post, they were certainly contributory concerns.

The church's responsibility within the employment of a youth worker is an area that would benefit from further research. This would enhance existing church-based youth work and help churches seeking to employ a youth worker avoid many of the pitfalls indicated in this research. Whilst Cliff may not be in a position to provide sufficient full-time training in the specific field of youth ministry (the YMM being a part-time course), from the findings of this study there is potential for Cliff to provide the foundational tools required. There is a potential wealth of knowledge, life-changing experiences and spiritual enrichment in full-time undergraduate study at Cliff College. What must be recognised by staff and students is that full-time youth ministry is not an easy option, nor is it something that anyone can do. Youth ministry requires the call of God, specific training, Christ-like attitude and sustained spirituality on behalf of the youth worker.

Recommendations

The purpose of this research was to facilitate the equipping of Cliff graduates for full-time church-based youth ministry. The results and analysis of this study indicate the following recommendations may significantly improve preparation of graduates and subsequent effectiveness in ministry:

- Increased training in inter-personal skills
- Accurate understanding of the role's requirements
- Support scheme for graduates in their first year of youth ministry

These could be incorporated into the existing timetable, helping graduates succeed in their first appointment in full-time church-based youth ministry. Outline proposals presented here are attainable and a step towards Cliff as a training institution better preparing graduates.

The following suggestions would involve further development of certain modules within the taught programme at Cliff and within the mission and placement structure. These developments should be options within the compulsory structure, only for those students seeking to pursue full-time church-based youth ministry. These suggestions could be used as a pilot project, evaluated at a later date by participant students subsequently employed by churches as full-time youth workers. The comparison of a similar study to this in ten years time would be insightful and beneficial.

Aim 1:

To Increase Training in Inter-Personal Skills in Relation to Youth Ministry

Action:

Incorporate into the existing academic programme, throughout Levels One to Three, the importance of effective, working relationships within ministry, specifically youth ministry as researched here. This should be delivered in greater depth than has been customary over the last decade. As the findings in this research suggest, relationships as experienced on short-term missions and placements do not sufficiently prepare students for the relational aspects of full-time youth ministry. A shift towards weekly, local placements on a long-term basis could improve this and give students a more realistic picture of the importance of good relationships with other leaders, ministers, parents and young people. In addition, students would learn experientially ways of handling conflict and perhaps the pitfalls of poor handling of conflict situations.

Aim 2:

Facilitate an Accurate Understanding of Full-Time Church-based Youth Ministry

Action:

Specifically for students pursuing full-time youth ministry, long-term placements should be established with local churches, ideally alongside a full-time youth worker, to facilitate realistic practical youth ministry experience. Students should be regularly assessed to aid development of skills and understanding of the principles and practice of full-time youth ministry. Students would choose these placements rather than making them obligatory, the fundamental purpose of these placements being to help equip students considering full-time youth ministry.

In addition to the suggested regular practical experience, there would also be a Leavers' Course delivered within the second semester each year. This would comprise five ninety-minute sessions, focussing on generic issues in church-based ministry, particularly for those in their first posts. These sessions would cover employment law, employer expectations, leadership and management theories, handling conflict and other associated issues. Specialists from a variety of full-time lay ministries would be incorporated into this course, including those in full-time youth ministry.

Aim 3:
Facilitate a Graduate Support Scheme for the First Year in Youth Ministry
Action:
This research shows that the suggestion of an annual Forum Day for those employed in full-time youth ministry would be helpful and potentially well supported. This could operate on a similar basis to the existing Forum held biannually at Cliff for Methodist Evangelists. Experienced practitioners would deliver relevant training in youth ministry, encouraging fresh thinking and new ideas for graduate youth workers. There would be time for spiritual reflection, enabling essential revitalisation for mission and ministry. The forum would also facilitate helpful networking and support for graduates away from their employment.

An optional mentoring scheme would be available to assist graduates in their first year of youth ministry. The value of mentoring was noted by one interview respondent, who emphasised the importance of having 'someone you trust who's outside of your work situation, who you can talk to, and ask for advice.'[4] A mentor would be arranged for each graduate requesting involvement in the scheme. Established youth workers with at least three years experience, ideally also Cliff graduates, would mentor new youth workers in their first year of employment. This system would provide consistent support from someone sufficiently removed from the graduate's employment situation, who could offer wise counsel or simply a listening ear. These mentoring relationships could potentially be continued beyond the initial year, providing long-term friendship and support.

To engage in ministry amongst young people today is one of the most vital elements of the Church's mission. 'Young people are beloved by God and are his instruments for bringing change and

---

[4] Graduate Interview 3, Appendix C, p.99.

renewal to the Church.'[5] Those called to, 'help young people discover and grow in their faith are therefore central to the continued witness of the church in this country.'[6] This high estimation of the calling to full-time church-based youth ministry should be acknowledged and embraced by Cliff and those whom God has called to this work, and as much as possible should be done to facilitate successful and effective youth ministers.

---

[5] Ward, *Growing up,* p.221.
[6] Ward, *Growing up,* p.221.

Appendix A

Focus Group Discussion Extracts

Date: 12 March 2005

Focus Group members:
Myself as researcher and discussion facilitator;
5 Cliff graduates who left Cliff between 1996 and 2004 and entered full-time, church-based youth ministry;
2 Cliff students, who had expressed an interest pursuing full-time, church-based youth ministry after graduating;
Group assistant, who recorded the discussion.

Discussion Extracts

1.   **What led you to be involved in working with young people?**

I've always enjoyed working with young people...I was the youth leader at my church for about three years before I went to Cliff, I knew the year before I actually started at Cliff that God was calling me into full-time youth work. I went to Cliff because I knew I needed some training before I could do this.

I had absolutely no idea what I would do after I left Cliff. I came here because I felt it was the right thing to do, but I didn't come expecting to go into full-time youth work, not at all. In fact, I never really thought I was any good with young people. It was only through the missions and Derwent week, when I was involved in the youth work that I ever seriously thought youth work was where God was leading me.

I'd had some involvement with young people, but I too did not ever really think youth work was where I was heading. To be honest, I had no idea what I would do after Cliff. I guess I knew God wanted me to do some sort of ministry type work, I knew I wouldn't be going back to my old job, but other than that I was completely open to wherever the Lord led me...I think I kind of stumbled into youth work...Yes, it was kind of a gradual thing for me...a friend of mine had been a student at Cliff and she loved it...it was mainly her recommendation of the place that encouraged me to come here...we'd also had a Cliff mission years before when I became a Christian...the youth worker at my church was fantastic...he wasn't full-time or anything, but I think he kind of inspired me for youth work...I got involved with helping out when I was about 21, and I guess it was a progression from that really that I came to the point of wanting to serve God working full-time with young people.

2. What sorts of things motivate you for youth ministry and make working with young people enjoyable?

I guess working with young people keeps you energetic...it's a fun job in lots of ways...

I don't think you could ever describe working with young people as boring...I think the motivation comes from seeing changes happen in young peoples lives, and knowing that you've been a part of that...I sometimes feel like I'm still a kid myself in some ways, I enjoy the same kind of stuff that young people enjoy...it sometimes doesn't feel like work. I agree, but I think it depends on the kind of person you are and the particular job you're doing. I mean, I'm a lot older so I don't see what I do in the same way as perhaps a younger youth worker might do. For me, it does feel like work. I don't see anything wrong with that though, because at the end of the day, I'm being paid to do a job, so why should it feel like something other than work?

I think the whole 'is this work, or is this ministry?' question is a crucial aspect of what we do. I know what you mean about it feeling like work, but I don't describe what I do as work, I describe it as ministry, because work stops and starts, whereas ministry should be a way of life...The danger with that is that as youth workers, we can become doormats, and the whole adage of churches having unrealistic expectations can come into this whole debate. We are paid to do a job, just like anyone else. There's a huge difference between lay workers, which is effectively what we are and ordained ministers. The thing that motivates me for working with young people is the knowledge that God has called me to this work.

3. How did you find your first year in full-time, church-based youth ministry?

The first year was great, for me. It was the second year that I found difficult. It was like the honeymoon period was over, and reality set in. My line manager started talking about long-term goals for the youth work and stuff. I felt a bit out of my depth to be honest. It was like I was suddenly doing a management job or something. I found that hard to cope with. I sometimes felt a bit of a fraud, to be honest, I knew I felt out of my depth with some things, but I guess I just wanted to show them I could do the job, even though I couldn't. It was weird, I just didn't want to admit I was struggling I suppose, showing my weaknesses and stuff. I thought I'd be ok, but at times I really wasn't, and I didn't know anyone well enough to share how I was feeling.

I felt the same, in many ways. I think looking back, I was still quite young and it felt like a huge jump from being a student to doing the job that I did when I left Cliff. I wasn't that much older than a lot of the young people I was working with, and in some ways they were more mature than I was! Yes, I agree with that. I think if I was in that job now, being a few years older, I would have handled things far better.

The first six months for me were brilliant. Like what was said earlier, it didn't really feel like work at times. I think, looking back I wasn't as disciplined as I should have been, and I kind of got into a pretty lazy routine of getting up late and going to bed late, and so on. Maybe that's why it didn't feel like work sometimes. Working from home didn't help either...it was all too easy to just do what I needed to do for the various clubs, assemblies or whatever, then just kick back and relax. I wish I'd had an office to actually go to, rather than working in my flat...I think you're right there, I did work from an office at the church, and that really helped me to distinguish between what was work time and what was my time...I think particularly when you've just come straight from being a student, you're still in that mode of I can just roll out of bed when I want to, sort of thing...things must be a lot more easy going here now compared to when I was here...we were woke up at a ridiculous time, and had to be at prayers at 7.45am otherwise we had to see the Principal.

I think for me, because I'd worked full-time as a classroom assistant before I went to Cliff, I knew that it was important to do what I was being paid to do. One of the staff at Cliff used to say 'work when you work, play when you play, and don't confuse the two.' I found that to be really helpful.

My management group were quite controlling, which often made me feel under pressure and I guess a bit threatened sometimes... like they didn't fully trust me or something. That was hard to cope with...I just didn't see eye to eye with the minister. He always gave the impression that he knew best, and that his way was always right. He wasn't very supportive or encouraging most of the time.

Something else I really struggled with in that first year was just missing being at Cliff. I never thought I'd feel like that because I couldn't wait to leave! I really missed my mates and just the level of support you get in a place like this. I was on the phone nearly every night to my best mate from college...that was much harder than I thought it would be.

I found that it wasn't the young people, or the work I did with them that was difficult, but church members. A lot of them were parents of the kids I worked with, and it was like they expected miracles or something. They were always on my back for stuff, which got really annoying...I loved working with the young people, but I hadn't fully appreciated how much other work within the church I would be expected to do...The job was much harder than I thought it would be.

4.   In what ways did you feel prepared or unprepared for your first full-time position after leaving Cliff?

I think Cliff was good in some ways, like going on mission was helpful, but I don't think it really gave me any idea of what working as a full-time youth worker would really be like...Cliff gave me loads of ideas for things. Someone said to us that when you leave Cliff, you leave with kind of a carrier bag full of ideas for assemblies, youth groups and stuff. When you start your job as a youth worker, it's like you use up all of the ideas out of the bag, then realise that you've run out of stuff to do. That's when it really hit me how unprepared for that job I actually was. That was when I started to learn about full-time youth work...Yes, that's a really good way of describing it. I felt just like that. I'm not a great ideas person, either, so I felt terrified that I just wouldn't have a clue what to do after I'd used all the stuff I'd done at Cliff.

I used to feel a bit intimidated because the volunteers seemed to have loads more ideas for stuff than I did...they just seemed like they knew what they were doing a lot more too. It felt a bit weird, because I was the one paid to do the work with the young people, but they were better than me in lots of ways.

I think being at Cliff taught me things about faith and doctrine at a level I'd never known before...that was helpful in terms of working in a church...you need to know things about the Bible and theology at a deep level, and Cliff was good in that respect...I found the lectures really challenging and informative...I think what we needed more of was specific teaching about what it means to be a full-time youth worker. We had some lectures on youth work, and they were good for what they were intended for, for missions and things, but there are so many other really important aspects to being in full-time youth work that we were never told about...how are you meant to do a job when it feels like people are talking a totally different language, and you've got absolutely no idea what they are on about? Yes, I agree...there are loads of management type things that you need to be clued up on as a full-timer, but when you're in your first job straight after college, it all feels really scary, like you're a little fish in a great big ocean.

I found Cliff helpful for preparing me for youth work, especially through the missions...I was fortunate because I did quite a few missions that had a youth emphasis, if it hadn't been for these I think I would have felt really unprepared for work as a youth worker.

5.   What advice would you give to Cliff graduates entering full-time church based youth ministry?

Unless you're really sure it's the right thing for you, that God has actually called you to work with young people, don't do it! I know of loads of people who were at Cliff at the same time as I was, who applied for youth work jobs often because they just didn't know what else they could do...they needed a job, youth work jobs seemed to pay better than some other lay work jobs, so they applied for them, and many of them got the job. It used to make me really annoyed, because I knew that they just weren't right for working with young people...a lot of them left their jobs within a year, it's all so tragic really.

I think my advice to someone at Cliff who was considering going into full-time youth work would be to look into getting some specific training and experience. There are loads of places around now where you can spend a year training as a youth worker, and just seeing if it's the right move...it's kind of a similar model to Foundation Training, where you can spend time seriously discerning if something is right. I think youth work and ministry is just as important as ordained ministry, so why shouldn't you spend as much time discerning whether it's right or not?

I think one of the differences is that the person involved doesn't have to pay themselves to do Foundation Training, but with some of the courses in youth work, they would have to pay to do them...when you've just left Cliff already owing thousands of pounds, you just can't afford more debt, what you need is a job...you're right when you said before that the whole finance issue is a huge motivation for applying for a youth work job.

I also know quite a few people who didn't stay long in their first job as youth workers, simply because the job was just too big for them...I'd advise anyone leaving Cliff, unless they've had quite a bit of experience in youth work already, to apply for 'smaller' jobs, in just one church for example...not huge circuit youth worker posts, where you need big time management skills as well as being able to do the job of working with young people...there are definitely some youth work positions that are just not 'first jobs'. I think this is where Cliff needs to be more proactive in advising students on which jobs to apply for, and why...what the differences are, and things like that...There are some youth work jobs that are good for learning the trade of youth work – gaining experience so that you're in a better position to do a bigger job a few years down the line. That's a good point, when I left Cliff I knew I wanted a job that I was pretty sure I could handle, rather than going for ones that looked really difficult, I went for, as you describe – 'smaller jobs'...ok, so the salaries weren't as big, but I knew that I wanted to start off small. I worked at a church I'd been to on a mission, and I knew kind of what they were after from a youth worker, and like I say, I felt I could cope with it. It was good for me; I kind of cut my teeth in youth work in that job... I stayed for three years, then moved on to a bigger, more demanding job...if I'd have gone straight into that job from Cliff, I definitely wouldn't have lasted long. This whole issue of the right job at the right time is crucial, in my opinion.

Something else that I know I messed up a number of times is in the area of working relationships with church people, stewards, and other people in the church where I was working. I was young and thought I knew it all when it came to youth work. I wish I'd had the humility to learn from other people, and sometimes just take criticism on the chin a bit more...I guess no one likes to be told they've made a mistake, but looking back, I know I made hundreds and couldn't take it when someone pointed them out to me...I think I'd say to people to learn from others, and not to be so arrogant or afraid to admit your own mistakes.

6.   Question to Cliff Students – Why are you considering full-time church based-youth ministry after you graduate?

I've felt called to work full-time with young people for a number of years now...about two years before I came to Cliff as a student, I was working in retail full-time and involved with the youth work at my home church...a few people had said I'd be good as a full-time youth worker, and suggested going to study at Cliff College to learn more about full-time ministry. I was involved in youth work at the Festival in my second year, and God has been confirming to me that it is definitely what I should be doing when I leave here.

I came to Cliff originally just for one year, to take a year out after my A levels. I've ended up staying here for three years, which I never expected to do. It's been good though, and although I've not done that much youth work before coming here, I've really enjoyed working with kids on mission and at Festival. I'm not sure whether I'm more of a children's worker or a youth worker though...I feel pretty confident at both, but there are some big differences between children and young people...listening to all that's been said here today, it's made me realise that I need to be sure about what I'm doing and why I'm doing it...it's difficult though. You've given me a lot to think about...Yes, me too...I'd be interested in finding out where I could do some proper training in youth work, maybe doing something as well as working as a youth worker...I think CYM (Centre for Youth Ministry) do courses that you do as part of a job, don't they? Yes, they do, that would be a great introduction to full-time youth ministry.

Appendix B

Questionnaire Results

Questionnaire One

<u>Please complete and return as soon as possible to:</u>

Sue Peat, Cliff College, Calver, Hope Valley, Sheffield, S32 3XG

Or contact me via email / telephone –
Email: s.peat@cliffcollege.org   Tel: 01246 584208

Name...

How old where you when you left Cliff College? (please tick)

19–25	26–35	36–45	Over 45
12	24	8	11

Collation of returned responses:

Full-time, Church-based Youth Ministry (0)

Ministerial Training (3)

Church Lay Work (12)
Lay work **6**
Children's work **3**
Voluntary mission work overseas **2**
Evangelist **1**

Para-Church Organisation (2)
Christian Aid **1**
YFC Worker **1**

Further training/education (please specify) **(7)**
Teacher training (PGCE) **4**
MA at Cliff College **2**
Nursing training **1**

Secular Employment (18)
Returned to previous employment **5**
Care Assistant **2**
Hotel domestic work **2**
Shop assistant **2**
Building site labourer **1**
Care home **1**
Fast Food Restaurant **1**
Leisure Centre **1**
Secretarial **1**
Shop Assistant **1**
Supermarket work **1**

Other (13)
Unemployed (for over 6 months) **4**
Retired **3**
Got married **2**
Had children **2**
Looked after elderly mother **1**
Travelled **1**

Unreturned (19)

Questionnaire Two

Thank you so much for taking the time to complete this questionnaire. Your experiences and opinions are vital to the further improvements of Cliff College for the training and equipping of future students.

Name: ....

(Please note – all names will be kept confidential and will not be used in the dissertation. However, it will be helpful for me to know who you are in order to contact you if you could be of any further help to me with my research.)

Address: ....

Email: ....

Tel: ....

1. Which year(s) did you study full-time at Cliff College? (please tick)

95/96	96/97	97/98	98/99	99/00	00/01	01/02	02/03
2	7	10	11	12	10	8	6

03/04	04/05
2	2

2. How old were you when you left Cliff?

19–25	26–35	36–45	Over 45
22	8	0	0

3. For how many years had you been in full-time employment before studying at Cliff?

None	1–5	6–10	10+
19	8	3	0

4. How long after leaving Cliff did you begin work in full-time, church-based youth ministry?

Within 3 months | 3–6 months | 6–12 months
24 | **3** | **3**

5. How long were you / have you been employed in this position?

Less than 1yr | 1–2yrs | 2–3yrs | 3+ years
4 | **11** | **6** | **9**
(1 employed in original job) | (1 employed in original job) | | (5 employed in original job)

Currently still employed in this position
7

6. How long was your initial contract for?

1 Year | 2 Years | 3 Years | Other
0 | **5** | **22** | **3**

7. If you are no longer working in this post, what were your reasons for leaving?

Changed jobs (within church based youth ministry) **3**
Commenced ministerial training **2**
Changed jobs (still within church based work) **4**
Youth ministry training **1**
Other **13**
- Stress / depression **1**
- Couldn't cope with job, also father was ill **1**
- Contract came to an end, no more funds **2**
- Resigned due to poor management **1**
- Resigned due to unhappiness in the job **1**
- Had a second baby and gave up work **1**
- Did not see eye to eye with the church or my line manager **1**
- The job was not what I thought it was, left and was unemployed for 6 months **1**
- Bullied by the minister & some church stewards **1**
- Changed jobs (not church work) **3**

8. Did your employer offer you any further training specifically in youth ministry?

Yes   No
2006.   **17**

Please expand on this.

- Conferences mainly – useful for inspiration **1**
- Contact with other youth workers **1**
- Needed more help in sustaining myself personally / training **1**
- I didn't ask for any, but if I had it probably would have been provided. Most people only suggested training if it would directly benefit them, rather than be helpful to my development **1**
- Training I was offered was generally oriented towards time management, organisational skills, etc rather than youth work. **1**
- It was offered, but no action was taken **1**
- Specific training in youth work was not offered, but I sought my own further training – Oasis, Youthwork conference, IASYM **1**
- I would have liked some! **1**
- Ongoing training, conferences etc – worked as an intern with a fulltime youth worker at first **1**
- Spectrum course which was too basic for my needs
- Oasis youth ministry course – helped me to get to grips with current thinking and practice while working in the job, was also a good link with others doing similar work. Involved a lot of travel though. **1**
- Helped me keep up to date with current thought, method etc – was good to network with other youth workers **1**
- YFC national training – was very helpful **1**
- I knew the church well and they knew me – it all worked well for the time I was there
- Spectrum training course over 12 weeks – gave me insight into youth culture and how to relate on a personal level **1**

9. Do you feel there were sufficient support structures in place for you as an employee?

Yes   No
11   **19**

Please expand on this.

- I didn't have many outlets of support – people I could be real with and share deep emotional issues.
- I struggled during my time at Cliff, and maybe didn't make the right choice of going into full-time ministry.
- The post had been in existence for a good while before my employment, with previous Cliff graduates working there. The job was well established. My working hours weren't managed very well though.
- I didn't feel very supported and the church had unreal expectations.
- My role was well and carefully managed, giving me a basis from which to work. There is an underlying structure, but I have freedom for new ideas and initiatives. I have an excellent support group.
- My management group were excellent, really supportive.
- There was plenty of management, but little support.
- Over management was a problem at first – everyone on the management group had their own ideas about what I should be doing.
- I have a support structure, but it's quite unclear and seems to lack clear purpose.
- My boss was a control freak, and was only willing for me to report to him. There was no support group, except for two friends who were always supportive.
- I had no support. I was just expected to get on with the job on my own, come up with ideas, etc.
- I have a great management group that I meet with every three months. Young people are also on this panel.
- I also meet with a mentor every two months who is also a youth worker.
- I was part of a youth work team, there were lots of issues among the team – some were trained more than others and different opinions emerged. Management was not good.
- Met weekly with support group to pray and talk through plans etc
- When I started it took three years to get the right level of support, once this was sorted things improved.
- Sufficient structures, but they didn't work. The vicar was difficult to work with and we didn't agree on a number of things, our working relationship fell apart. The young people were great though.

- Support group was useful for airing thoughts and ideas and as a back up for contentious issues.
- It wasn't always easy having the minister as line manager and as my personal pastoral overseer.
- Management group were very controlling and had completely unreal expectations, personality clash between me and my line manager.
- The post was very well organised despite being quite hastily put together.
- The structures were there, but they weren't particularly supportive. I felt lonely and unsupported.

10. What experience of working with young people had you had before undertaking this post?

- Church voluntary youth work **18**
- Cliff Celebration/Derwent **13**
- Cliff Missions **24**
- 5 week 3rd year placement **2**
- Not very much at all **3**
- Easter People **1**
- Voluntary secular youth work **1**
- Share Jesus missions **2**
- Oasis trust missions **1**
- YFC experience **1**
- None **1**

11. Concerning the specific aspects listed below, how would you rate the preparatory training you received at Cliff for your first full-time post in church based youth ministry?

	Excellent	Very Good	Adequate	Poor
Spiritual	12	14	4	0
Theological	1	12	0	1
Organisation	5	13	9	3
Personal	4	16	9	1

	Excellent	Very Good	Adequate	Poor
Experiential	4	21	2	3
Creative	6	15	9	0
Relational	3	9	17	1

12. How do you feel Cliff could have prepared you better for work with young people?

- Teaching about how to cope in ministry **3**
- Practical help on how to manage time/admin **4**
- How to cope with personal issues / struggles **2**
- Long term placements **5**
- I didn't go to Cliff to train for work with young people **3**
- How to find the right job, how to know if the job being applied for is realistic in terms of expectations, etc **1**
- Careers, calling advice **3**
- Specific teaching on full-time youth work, starting out in youth work **3**
- How to relate to your superiors / peers **8**
- How to be a leader as a young person amongst young people **7**
- Specific youth work missions / placements. Most of my missions were great, but involved working with older people **3**
- Teaching on full-time youth work **3**
- There was no youth work option, as there is now. This would have been helpful. I had very little teaching on how you actually go about working with young people **3**
- It would have been helpful to work alongside full-time youth workers, particularly those who 'don't fit the mould' of a 'trendy' youth worker **1**
- I'm not sure. I think working with young people is one of those things that you learn more about when you're actually doing it, rather than just talking about it **1**
- I did the youth work option in my second year, which was good, but It would have been better if this teaching could have continued through to the third year **1**
- More specific placements **2**
- More specific training on practical issues like child protection, good practice etc **2**
- How to deal with conflict **1**

- Training on how long to keep trying in a difficult situation before it becomes damaging to you **1**
- Possible support in first job from college? **1**
- Not sure it could as I was only there for a year and it was mainly Bible-based study. If I had wanted specific youth training I would have chosen to go somewhere that specifically offered that. I wanted to be at Cliff for the Biblical studies and fellowship and to discern where God was leading – I didn't know at the start that it would be youth work **1**
- I left at Christmas in my second year because I felt I was not in the right place, I guess I would have got more from Cliff had I stayed, since the second year was more practical. I had a good foundation to build on. **1**
- Not sure **1**

13. I plan to set up interviews comprising of a cross section of questionnaire respondents. Please state if you would be willing to be interviewed. Involvement will entail one confidential interview with me for the purpose of gaining broader and deeper insight into the subject matter of this research.

Yes, I am willing to be interviewed   **27**

No, I am not willing to be interviewed   **3**

(Please note, not all respondents will be contacted)

14. Would you have been / would you be interested in attending an annual Forum Day for youth workers, based at Cliff providing support, training and fellowship?

Yes	No	Maybe
11	**5**	**14**

Many thanks for your help.

Please return in the envelope provided as soon as possible.

Sue Peat
Evangelist

Appendix C

Interview Transcripts

Interview I: Church Leader

Male, Methodist Minister

Date: 9 December 2006

1.   How long have you been a Methodist minister?

Twenty-six years.

2.   Within the last ten years, how many full-time church-based youth ministry appointments have you been involved in?

Three within the last ten years, though there have been others before that time which I think would be relevant to this research.

3.   What were the aims of these appointments?

I think the aims were slightly different with each appointment; however, generally the overall aim was to increase the effectiveness of the church with young people. Mostly the aim was to reach young people outside the church, but the exact job descriptions have varied quite a lot across the appointments.

4. Tell me a little about the work with young people here at this church, both within the last ten years, and currently

This church has a reputation for a strong emphasis on work with children and young people. Over the years, that has ebbed and flowed as happens in most churches. Currently I would say that the youth work is gaining in strength very much, and we're encouraged by that, but I think we've been through a period of three years where actually the youth work has been in some decline, or at least stagnant.

5. Why do you think that was?

Three years ago when we employed our last youth worker, the job description changed somewhat fairly early in the time of that employment. It's quite a long story in a way. What happened was that we were seeking to employ a lay worker. We had somebody in post who we interviewed for the continuation of her work. The panel who interviewed her were split as to whether to employ her again or not, but the majority of the panel favoured employing her, and we made that decision.

One of the biggest mistakes that we have made in these four years, was what happened the next day, which was one member of the panel came back to me and said, 'I think we should employ the other person as well.' We brought this to the church, and that proposal went through at the church council meeting. In other words, the church committed themselves to about an additional £17,000 of expenditure. Now that second appointment was not very well thought through, so we ended up employing both a lay worker and a youth worker, which for most churches is a great luxury. However, I was happy with that, and to start with things were ok. Then we had the opportunity to develop some new work on a housing estate, and the plans all went forward for this. We were looking to rent premises, and we had a lot of meetings with the local council, local schools, police and the community, and the youth worker's time was taken up with that to an extent which was unwise, in retrospect. At the point where we were about to launch the project, we were unable to do so because of local opposition within the community. We then found that we seemed to have gone down a large *cul-de-sac* on this, and the youth worker was highly committed to this work in the community, though to be honest, now I would say that he was not equipped to do that work.

Although at the time, I could not see why that work was being prevented. In God's plans, I can see it now. So we had everything lined up. All the money was in place, the church was in agreement, there was considerable enthusiasm in the church and in the community, but in the end, due to opposition in the vicinity of the area where we were planting this youth cell, we couldn't go ahead. Now after that adjustment had to be made, the youth worker somehow never adjusted to that, I think lost motivation and actually didn't have too many ideas. He didn't seem like he wanted to connect much with all the regular things that happen here week by week. He actually wanted to run his own project on his terms. This is all in retrospect. It wasn't this clear as this at that time.

What was needed, and the church now recognise this, was a management group for that youth worker, apart from myself as Minister and line manager, to say to him 'You need to plug in to the local church, because here we have 100 un-churched young people who come onto our premises every week, get involved there.' The youth worker did not want to do this, so he didn't go to any of the various uniformed organisations with any regularity, only occasionally. Then, the final frustration came when the Junior Church teachers, who are a very dedicated bunch of people, decided to do a monthly youth club on a Saturday night. The youth worker didn't go because he wanted to do his own social things. That went down extremely badly with the church, and in the end, that was the straw that broke the camel's back. So although we had adjusted the youth worker's job description to suit what he wanted to do, and improved his accommodation package, which he'd complained about, though actually in our view it was quite a generous package, at the point where those things were now favourable to him, he then handed in his notice.

It was a painful experience, and one that we've learned from, so that now we have a new lay worker, who actually has very great skills in youth work, and is a more experienced person altogether, we have a strong management group who work with him, in addition to myself. In fact I'm not on the management group, unless they specifically need me there. We realise now that many of the issues concerning the frustrations and lack of proper supervision of what the youth worker was actually doing with his time, should have been dealt with much sooner than they were.

6.   For how long was the youth worker employed here?

Two years and two months.

7.   When would you say that things began to 'go wrong' with his employment?

I think this happened for different people at different times. I think I was actually rather tolerant of the situation for at least 18 months. Others, including some on the staff were not at all tolerant of the situation because they saw a great deal of unfairness. The youth worker was doing very little real work, though there was lots of networking going on. He was there for the up-front stuff sometimes, but when it came down to the daily graft, and the consistent being there and working with people, that wasn't happening. So some people were really unhappy about this appointment after four to six months. As team leader, I was trying to keep all of this together, and share work out where possible. I would say that personally, my relationship with the youth worker was good for the great majority of the period of his employment, and it was only in about the last four months that it began to unravel, and then at the point when he handed in his notice it unravelled really quickly, because of the way that was done. There are lots of learning points in all this.

8.   How well did Cliff graduates present themselves in interviews?

They generally presented themselves quite well. When I was at Cliff on the staff, (1994–2002) it was said to me by a few people in local church leadership that Cliff students did not present themselves well at interview, nor did they give very good CV's. I don't think this was the case with the ones I've been involved in appointing, in fact up front presentation in the case of the youth worker I've been referring to was one of his greatest strengths, and was one of the things that kept a lot of people on the church council on board with the youth worker. He presented things quite well, and in a way that suggested everything was going fine, when in fact it wasn't.

9.   What sort of line management structures were in place for that particular youth worker?

We had a weekly staff meeting for all the staff here. In addition, I would meet with both the lay worker and the youth worker individually on a regular, though less frequent basis. There was always a slot in the church council meeting where the youth worker would give an account of what was going on. I think we needed a tighter accountability structure in this case, but in other cases that I've been involved in, I'd say we really did not need that.

10. Did the youth worker have a support group in addition to a line management group?

We're very blessed here with lots of retired ministers, and there was one in particular who the youth worker related well to, and talked with about things one to one. I think there were some other points of reference that this youth worker had which were outside of this area. This of course was fine, though I suspect that he was receiving advice from outside the setting in a way that was extremely unhelpful and undermining to us. I don't have precise evidence for this, but what I was hearing from the youth worker I thought I was hearing another person saying it. I was deeply unhappy about this.

11. Was further training in youth ministry offered to the youth worker?

Yes, there was always opportunity to go on courses and conferences. Some of those were local and some were national. We encourage that and we fund it for staff members.

12. How well do you feel the youth worker did during their term of employment?

In the case I've referred to, our youth work actually declined, and I have to say that since he's left, the youth work has taken off. When he was employed, I as Minister stepped back from much of the involvement with youth work, to allow him space to develop things himself. However, because some of the previous involvement I'd had was not taken up by the youth worker, we ended up with a bit of a void. Again, there was networking, but there was virtually no going out on the street talking to young people and making contact with un-churched kids. I think for a while I assumed this was happening, but it wasn't.

13. What were the positive aspects of this appointment?

This particular youth worker was very good at preaching and leading worship, and actually I think that was what he wanted to do. I don't think he was gifted in youth work. He was a young person himself, he'd got a degree from Cliff College, and in his early twenties, he assumed and we assumed that he was gifted in the area of youth work. I think that was a wrong assumption. I assumed that he was skilled in youth work and had more experience than actually he had. When it came down to it, he didn't really have that much experience in youth work at all. I overestimated his capabilities, and therefore gave him more scope to develop his own thing than was probably wise.

He needed more management than I gave to him and for that I blame myself. That's not to say he didn't get on with children and young people, he did. In fact, to some extent he was a hero to a few. What he didn't have was a desire to connect with un-churched young people on the whole, and that was a big part of the job description. He was keen to set up a project but then when that failed he didn't want to work alongside the leaders of the uniformed organisations within the church, and when you have large numbers of children coming to those groups, whether you like it or not, that's a big part of youth work. Some of what he did was good work, it's just that when I look back, I feel as if we should have done things quite differently, and the management of his employment should have been better.

One of the first things that the youth worker did when he started the job was to close down a new youth group that had been established for un-churched youngsters. I should have realised that that was a warning sign, because that happened without any proper consultation with me, I just discovered afterwards that a decision had been made. Now, it was not a thriving work, but it was reaching a handful of un-churched youth. He said he didn't want to work that way, but I never found out what the alternative route was. He'd had some previous experience with a very large, progressively thinking church elsewhere, and he felt that their model of youth work was the best way forward, and wanted to operate a similar model here. Well, that's simply not where we are here, and I'm not convinced that's the best model anyway, necessarily. So I think we needed to have done some deconstruction on that very specific model of youth work. He deconstructed some aspects of the existing youth work here, but he never replaced them with something else. There was a Cell Group though, which only met sometimes.

14.   Do you think that formal support structures from Cliff, both for the graduate and for the church, would have been helpful in the first year of employment?

I think it's very difficult to answer that question because a lot depends on the personality of the person you're dealing with. I think there needs to be a letting go of Cliff College on the part of the individual. I welcome the trend that's being developed at Cliff of the Student Evangelist, as I can see that as a really excellent stepping stone to local church ministry.

15.   Any other comments?

I think there needs to be a greater emphasis on placements within the college programme, and less on missions. This is something I tried to develop in my time there, so that students leave college and enter church-based ministry situations with a more realistic idea, and are willing to accept the situation as it is, and not as they would want it to be. Also, that they hang in there, even though things may not be perfect. We've had a very recent situation where a Cliff student was appointed as a youth worker at one of the churches in the circuit, and only stayed in the job five weeks. Everyone thought this was the right person for the job, he had the skills, all the relationships were good, and yet the guy left after five weeks, leaving the churches in a mess really. We've been able to cover with sessional work, which to be honest is actually working quite well.

Interview II: Church Leader

Female, Methodist Minister

Date: 14 October 2006

1.   How long have you been a church leader?

Fifteen years.

2.   Within the last ten years, how many full-time church-based youth ministry appointments have you been involved in?

Just the one.

3.   **What was the aim of the appointment?**

The work with young people was growing, which was really encouraging, but at the time, (1998) we didn't really have anyone who could properly commit to working with the kids, so we spent some time thinking and praying about it, and decided to look into employing a youth worker. I think the aim was really to develop the work that was already going on. We were doing our best, though none of the people involved felt equipped to do this work really. Some of the young people who came to the youth club were pretty demanding and hard work!

4.   **Tell me a little about the work with young people here; both within the last ten years, and currently**

I've been here for nine years and there have always been children and young people connected with the church in some way, either through Junior Church, Brownies and Guides or the Friday night Youth Club. I'm not the greatest when it comes to working with kids, but there have generally been a couple of people who see youth work as their ministry. There are more people involved with the young peoples work now than for a good few years. I think this is in some ways because of what the youth worker did while he was here in building up not only the work, but some leaders as well. We now have two groups that meet every week, one is a group for young people wanting to know more about God, kind of like a discipleship group; the other is the one that's been running for years on a Friday night, where they can play table tennis, football, etc. There's also Brownies, Guides and a group on Sunday mornings for young people. This is for kids who've grown too old for Junior Church but don't want to sit through the whole of the church service.

5.   **Can you explain the overall processes that eventually led to the full-time youth worker appointment?**

We realised we needed some help and we had a sense of vision for the youth work, there's such great potential here location wise. We had most of the funding in place when we advertised, but not all of it. I talked with a few other churches and Ministers who'd employed youth workers, just to get their advice really on how to go about it. We decided we'd employ someone for one year, and then see how it went from there. By the time we interviewed the candidates, all the money was there. We really believed God was in this right from the start. We interviewed three people, all of whom were good candidates, but he just stood out to us as the right one. We offered him the job and he accepted it.

6. How well did the Cliff graduate present himself in the interview?

He came across very well. He was confident, answered the questions thoughtfully and with reasonably good knowledge. We liked him from the start of the interview.

7. What sort of line management structures were in place for the youth worker?

His line manager was one of the Stewards in the church, who'd had some previous experience of youth work line management. I felt that I should not be the line manager, as in a sense I was also going to be his Pastor, as he would also be a church member. He and his line manager met once a month to talk through plans and evaluate how things had gone that month. He also had a support group, made up of people in the church who he met with and who prayed for him and the young people's work on a regular basis. I also met with him every week for prayer.

8. How long was the probationary period?

Three months.

9. Was further training in youth ministry offered to the youth worker?

He went to a conference every year, and other local training days.

10. How well do you feel the youth worker did during their term of employment?

He actually stayed for two years. He did so well in that first year; we got more funding for him to stay another year. He had loads of enthusiasm for the young people and the kids absolutely loved him. He used to go into schools doing assemblies and a Rock Solid club that he started up; he really gave things a kick start in lots of ways. I know he found some parts of the job really challenging and difficult, particularly at first. There weren't many people his age at that time in the church, so he struggled to make any real friends for a while. I think this gradually improved as he got to know people more and made some links with other local youth workers. He was just a great asset to the church. One thing that he did that has had long term benefits was that he enabled others to be involved. People that you'd never have believed would do youth work, got involved in things and found out that they actually enjoyed it! I've heard stories of some youth workers, who out of their enthusiasm and desire for things to change have often been judgemental and arrogant in their approach with church people. This usually makes people dig their heels in even more! He was never like this. The old people loved him as much as the young people did. He just had a really great way with everyone he worked with.

11.   Do you feel that he was ready for the role of youth worker immediately after leaving Cliff College?

That's difficult to answer. I think so. I'm not sure how much of the success of his work was as a direct result of being at Cliff or just because of who he was as a person. I know he talked to me about feeling inadequate for the job at times. He'd not had that much experience of working with young people, particularly kids that don't behave how you'd like them to. I think he'd got a good grounding though at Cliff. He always spoke very fondly of his time there.

12.   With the benefit of hindsight, what issues has this appointment made you more aware of as an employer?

I don't think I've ever thought of myself as an employer really! I suppose you could say that though, in some ways. There's certainly a lot more involved than I think I'd first anticipated. I know I was very glad of church members and other Ministers who knew more about this whole thing than I did. It was a steep learning curve for me. I think if I was doing it again, or could turn the clock back, I'd have picked up on the fact that he must have felt pretty lonely – new place, new church, new job, new people, etc. I think that responsibility to the employee in this kind of work is really important. I'm glad he had people he could talk to about things openly, honestly and confidentially.

13.   Do you think that formal support structures from Cliff, both for the youth worker and for the church, would have been helpful in the first year of employment?

Yes, I think that would have been a good idea. It's a big difference going from college straight into church ministry. I think for the youth worker particularly, he would have valued having some sort of support form someone at Cliff in that first year. I have a feeling he missed the level of support he'd previously had at Cliff.

14.   Any other comments?

Employing a full-time youth worker was one of the best decisions this church have ever made. God has really given people here passion and vision for working with young people. There's talk at the moment about taking on a full-time worker again, as things are developing more and more with the young people, which is really encouraging.

Interview III: Graduate

Male
21 years old when graduated, no previous employment experience

Currently still in initial youth ministry post

Date: 15 October 2006

1.   How long have you been employed in full-time church-based youth ministry?

One year.

2.   What is it about working with young people that motivates you?

For me, it's the satisfaction of seeing young people grow up and develop both spiritually and emotionally, in spite of their own issues and difficulties. Certainly working on a council estate, I see this day in, day out. Some of the young people I work with really struggle to deal with things, but I think seeing young people, some of whom I know have not had it easy in life, doing things like passing their exams, going on to college or getting a job doing something they actually want to do, these things all are continual sources of motivation to me. Also, working in church-based youth work, and having the opportunity to share the Gospel with young people, is such a privilege and again, motivates me in all I do in my work.

3.   What led you to apply for this post?

During my second year at Cliff, I came to this church as part of a team for three blocks of time as part of a year long mission. The church had just recently bought a Spar shop on a council estate in Sheffield and I was privileged to be part of the move from being a church that worshipped in a school hall once a week, into their own property on a council estate. During my third year, I came back one Sunday morning to the church here. The minister came over to chat to me and said he'd really like to talk more with me about something. I met him a couple of weeks later and he shared with me that the church were looking to employ a youth worker. At that time, I felt that God was calling me to work with young people full-time, so we talked and prayed some more, and here I am.

4.   You mentioned that you felt God was calling you into youth ministry, can you expand on that a little please?

I think like a lot of students who leave Cliff, I started a job and in the first couple of weeks thought, 'Help! What am I doing here? This is too big for me.' But gradually, as I've got to know people and done my part in settling into the life of another church, I've kind of found my feet, got on with the job in hand, I've then seen God at work in what I've been doing and in what I'm part of. This has really confirmed that I am in the right place, and that this is what I've been called by God to do at this time.

5.   Tell me a little about the church with which you work

It was originally a House Church a number of years ago, then started meeting in a local school hall until about five years ago. There are currently about 160 people, including about 30 children and young people, all of whom are attend regularly. We're quite an informal church I guess, in terms of worship style. We're part of the Evangelical Alliance, though we're not connected with any formal denomination.

6.   What led them to appointing a youth worker?

The church had previously employed a youth worker some years ago, but there had been some serious problems, which resulted in the termination of his contract. After that, the church simply tried to continue the youth work without a paid employee but they realised that they really needed someone with a bit more experience and ideas, etc. They ended up with me!

7.   What are your responsibilities as youth worker?

There are currently some changes occurring to my job in terms of responsibilities. There is a serious divide between the young people in the church who come from the more middle class homes, and the young people on the estate where the church building situated. So my job is kind of expanding now to incorporate the young people here on the estate, which is great.

8.   Do you feel these are acceptable?

Yes, I welcome these changes.

9.   What does your work actually involve, week to week?

A standard week would involve church on Sunday, at which I run youth sessions part way through the service. Sunday evenings usually involves some sort of group or youth event, if not here, then at another local church that we have links with. A number of churches in this area do Sunday evening youth events, and we tend to support each other in these.

Monday is normally preparation time for me. Then we have a youth drop in for the kids on the estate on Monday nights, held at the Church.

Tuesdays are spent mostly working in a Primary School on the estate, I run an After School Club there for years 4 – 6. It's a completely Christian based club, and I guess part of my agenda is to get to know these kids so that when they move up into secondary school, there's already some connection with them – they know me, etc.

Wednesdays I'm usually in the local secondary school. I take assemblies, RE lessons and lunchtime clubs.

Thursday is my day in the office, so if anyone from church wants to pop in for a chat, see me about anything or whatever, I'm there for them.

Friday is my day off. Saturdays are kind of free too, but we quite often have something going on with church that I'll be involved in on a Saturday.

10.   How does your line management structure work?

It's kind of a bit hit and miss in some ways, but basically I meet with
one of the church members and the Minister's wife, at least once every
half term. These two people are my official line mangers. We look at
aims and objectives, my action plan for the next weeks and months. In
addition to this, we have regular phone calls, email contact to discuss
any issues that have arisen. The Minister used to be my line manager,
but because he was on sabbatical when I was first taken on, his wife,
was the one who appointed me, so he suggested that she and another
person from the church be the people that actually form my line
management.

11.   Do you feel supported by the church leaders / members?

Yes, I do feel supported, but it just seems a bit like messy support, if
you know what I mean. I have a team of five other people that work
with me in what I do with the young people, and they are really great.
Also, the rest of the church have been so committed to the work with
young people. One couple in the church very quickly noticed that early
on my wife and I were struggling, not to fit in, but to make any real
friends in the church. They invited us round for meals and really made
the effort to get to know us as a couple, not just as the youth worker
and his wife. Since then, we've both felt much more part of the family
of the church here.

**12.   Do you feel that your time as a student at Cliff College
sufficiently prepared you for your work here? Please
explain**

My gut reaction is to say no. As I mentioned earlier, when I started
here, for the first couple of weeks, all I could think was 'Help! How on
earth am I going to cope with this?' I didn't feel prepared for this job
really. Cliff was really good as an academic institution. I learnt a lot
about theology and the Bible and evangelism, but with the exception of
my third year placement, the practical aspect of the course, the missions
were either weekends or for ten days. I don't feel they were long
enough to experience in any great depth what it's actually like to be in
full-time ministry.

   Also, life at Cliff revolves very much around the Cliff
community, and that can become like a bubble; very inward looking,
very isolated from the outside world. I don't think that's a very healthy
thing to be honest. To go from that extreme to working for a church in a

wider community, working with people who have lives outside of church, who have other priorities and so on, and to generally find yourself in a situation that's very different to life at Cliff is a big deal, and again I wasn't prepared for that huge change.

13.   Specifically, what did Cliff prepare you for?

Being at Cliff gave me a good foundation for organisation. Working to deadlines, having to follow timetables, etc. has really helped me in my work here. Also, Cliff made me realise the vital need for worship and spirituality. During my third year, I was the music co-ordinator for the Class meetings, and that helped me appreciate the need for a worship structure, both personally and within ministry. Generally, the life and rhythm of college life helped me in my own walk with God, and that structure and discipline I still find helpful.

14.   And what do you feel it did it not prepare you for?

As I said earlier, at Cliff there's so much emphasis on 'the community', you find yourself really depending on people in a very strong way, in a way most people in normal life don't do. Some people in my year could be very draining on others when they were having what they thought was a huge crisis. It was like they couldn't cope unless certain other students were constantly there for them. Life just isn't like this, most of the time. You just have to get on with it, and maybe learn to trust God a bit more, instead of this great dependence on others. Ministry I've found can sometimes be a lonely road, and I really missed having lots of friends and like-minded people around to talk to, share with and so on.

Also, the missions, while they were good experiences in lots of ways, we weren't really ever in situations where we as students had to relate to church leaders or ministers. Similarly, if someone in the church was annoying or irritating, we knew that in a few days time, we'd be on our way back to Cliff! This didn't teach us about working through tricky situations, and treading carefully with what we said, because if it did all go pear shaped, we weren't going to have to face those people again. Full-time church based youth ministry is not like that. If I mess up, I do have to face that person again. So in that respect, I don't feel that Cliff prepared me for some parts of my job here.

98

15.   How do you feel Cliff could better prepare students for church-based youth ministry?

To start with, there needs to be more careers advice built into the course as a whole. In my third year, we had a fifteen minute tutorial with one of the tutors, and that was it. Thankfully I'd got this job by then, but there were people in my year who didn't really know what their options were, and would probably have benefited from some proper careers advice.

I always saw Cliff as a place I was called to go 'through', not just called 'to'. I think that's an important distinction, and if I was a tutor I would be stressing that, and asking the question – 'What are you going to do when you leave here?' Now I know that for some people continues to be a difficult question, because they just don't know. They've been obedient to God in going to Cliff, and are waiting for Him to show them the next step. But I do think that for the college to be as passive as I feel it is regarding what students do when they leave, is not very helpful.

16.   With the benefit of hindsight, are there things you would have done differently, either as a student at Cliff or now as a youth worker?

Well I don't have any regrets. I loved my time at Cliff, and I'm reasonably happy with the way this last year's gone. With hindsight, I would have taken the Evangelism and Young People module in my second year!

17.   Would you have benefited from some external support from Cliff during your first year in youth ministry?

Yes, this would have definitely been helpful. I think somehow by the grace of God I've coped this year. It's not been easy, but I've got through my first year and lived to tell the tale. I know others who've been through Cliff who haven't been so fortunate. Now maybe I'm a stronger character or can cope with things more than some, but I think some sort of contact from college would have been good. I think rightly or wrongly, there's an assumption that the staff at college are so busy with the students they've got, that there would be no time or opportunity for help and contact for ex-students.

Interview IV: Graduate

Male
21 years old when graduated, no previous employment experience

No longer in initial youth ministry post

Date: 18 November 2006

1. How long were you employed in full-time church-based youth ministry?

Two years and two months.

2. What is it about working with young people that motivates you?

There is something special about young people. They are honest and struggling; they're what the church should be; they're co-dependent. Also young people get Christianity; they understand that it's hard work; they understand that what Jesus asks is ridiculous and they understand that faith is hard work and that lying about all this is pointless.

3. What led you to apply for the post?

It felt natural. It was how Cliff worked. The expectation was that you graduate and either do a PGCE, ministerial training, or some sort of church-based job – usually youth work or lay work. There was an environment of expectation. I did enjoy youth work, though so I shouldn't complain too much; I just wish that I had gained the qualifications (e.g. JNC) to pursue youth work in a professional context (e.g. statutory sector) rather than in the church.

4. Tell me a little about the church with which you worked

The Methodist Church I worked for is a well-respected, large, traditional evangelical church. It is middle class to the core. What really set the church apart though was its work mentality. The rich congregation coughed up each week with the expectation that the employees should do the work. The Minister reinforced this ideology by seriously overworking and expecting his staff to do likewise. The pyramid structure was unreal; the Minister was the boss and we were employed not because of our gifting but because he didn't have enough time to do everything.

5.   What led them to appointing a youth worker?

I applied for the lay worker post and didn't get it, but they saw I had qualities that could fill the gap in their Sunday congregation, i.e. with young people, and found the money.

6.   What were your responsibilities as youth worker?

My job was to improve expand the work of the church to reach more young people, filling the gap where a large number of teenagers had recently left.

7.   Did you feel these were acceptable?

No, because the appointment was a spur of the moment thing, the objectives weren't really thought through, along with the supervision and pastoral care for that matter.

8.   What did your work actually involve, week to week?

I was involved in Kids' Clubs, Uniformed Organisations and other youth activities. In particular, a structured Youth Club, a less structured Cell Group and the odd bit of detached work. I also took part in a monthly Youth Service.

9.   How did your line management structure work?

My line manager was the Minister of the church and was a total workaholic. He very rarely had a day off, and expected others to show the same level of commitment. The effect of this was that there was no work / life balance; my life was my work and there was little room for anything else. I had no non-church friends in the area, my relationship with my partner was damaged on several occasions and I rarely had chance to pursue my own interests. Perhaps my line manager would have been happy with the norm – 50+ hour weeks, with one day and one additional evening off a week. The problem was that I was not willing to meet that norm.

10.   Did you feel supported by the church leaders / members?

No. As I mentioned earlier, the church seemingly wanted to get as much out of me as they could. There was one infamous meeting with a church member, when he had clearly been briefed by the boss, when I was told in no uncertain terms that I should 'stop feeling sorry for myself' and not 'expect everything to go my way'. The dominant understanding of my role and the role of anyone involved in full-time church work was that I should work 9-5, like anyone else works 9-5 for their employer, and then give my time on top as this is my offering to the church.

11.   Did you feel that your time as a student at Cliff College sufficiently prepared you for your work with that church? Please expand on this

In some regard it did. Cliff missions were great. We did some valuable and dynamic work, especially on my placement at St. Tom's in Sheffield. I learnt how to deal with young people, what I did not learn during my time at Cliff was how to deal with the church and its leadership or the complexity of full-time ministry.

12.   Specifically, what did Cliff prepare you for?

I gained a lot of practice in relating to young people, preaching and leading youth worship services.

13.   And what do you feel it did it not prepare you for?

Young people are unfortunately just a small part of being a youth worker. A much bigger part is taken up with interacting with the wider church and its leadership. I felt very un-prepared for this. Through Foundation Training, those that went on to become Deacons or Presbyters had vocational training. They were encouraged to think through their calling and the impact it might have on their life. After leaving Cliff I felt like I was thrown in at the deep end. I could talk to young people, but what good is that when your boss makes you feel like you're useless?

14.   Why did you leave this job?

I wasn't prepared to be treated the way I was being treated by my line manager. His workaholic approach to ministry was unhealthy, but he expected the same from me and other staff members. There was just no work / life balance. In retrospect, the job was a mistake.

15.   How do you feel Cliff could better prepare students for church-based youth ministry?

The most important thing that was lacking was a theology of work. At Traidcraft, my current employer, there is a really strict work / life balance. You work 37 hours per week and that's it. If you work more you take the time off in lieu the following week or the week after that. There is a massive concern for staff welfare. At the church where I was employed there wasn't that concern. They wanted, probably with good intentions, to get as much out of their workers as possible, irrespective of the cost to them or their loved ones. Moreover, the pressure to work longer hours was given a spiritual spin, with the use of words like 'servant ministry' and 'sacrifice'. For this reason I needed a theology of ministry, and Cliff did not provide this. On the contrary in fact, the lifestyle of many of the Cliff staff supported the Protestant work ethic that suggests that the longer and harder you work for the church; the more God is pleased with you. I do not believe that to be true. It is an ecclesiocentric view of ministry that does not recognise that when I spend time with my fiancé because she is struggling, or when I go to the pub with my mates, that is as much a service to kingdom of God as going to another church meeting.

Prospective youth workers should be taught about their rights as employees of the church. The church where I was employed was bursting with money, hundreds of thousands of pounds in the bank, yet, it turns out, I was underpaid for the entire length of my service.

16.   With the benefit of hindsight, are there things you would have done differently, either as a student at Cliff or as a youth worker?

I would not have become a youth worker in the local church. I would have got a job and done youth work voluntarily, but when I left Cliff I was desperate for a job and naively believed that that had to be in the church.

17.   Would you have benefited from some external support from Cliff during your first year in youth ministry?

Perhaps. In one regard, I did. One of the Cliff tutors mentored me in my second and third year and we have kept in touch since and that was helpful; especially because he was older and wiser and had been a youth worker himself, and had a good theology of ministry. I guess this was helpful because it was natural. It would be difficult to enforce this support. In closing I think it is worth saying what a serious business this is. I quit my job as a youth worker over a year ago but I feel so hurt by church leaders that I am still reluctant to go back to church.

Interview V: Graduate

Female
24 years old when graduated, previous employment experience

No longer in initial youth ministry post

Date: 7 October 2006

1.   How long were you employed in full-time church-based youth ministry?

I was only in my post for six months. Two of those months I was off sick.

2.   What is it about working with young people that motivates you?

I like a challenge and working with young people is a challenge for anyone, they bring so much fun and sometimes heartache but its all great fun working with them and supporting them in everyday life.

3.   What led you to apply for the post?

I believe strongly that I am called by God to work with young people. The post seemed right at the time and the Curate who interviewed me seemed so up for having a youth worker and had so many ideas which were interesting. I felt I was ready to take on the challenge.

4.   Tell me a little about the church with which you worked

I worked for an Anglican church, with a huge congregation and many children and young people. They were very evangelical and wanted the best for the children and the youth. They had a strong Sunday school set up but nothing for the young people, which is why they wanted to appoint a youth worker. Although it was a big church with lots of people, they were stuck in the last century in terms of worship, preaching and evangelism. This was really frustrating, particularly after being at Cliff for three years. Nothing I said seemed to make any difference; it was like I was speaking a different language with some of them.

5.   What led them to appointing a youth worker?

It was the Curate who had a strong sense that they needed to employ a youth worker because there was no activities going on for the youth and they wanted someone to develop the ministry in the church.

6.   What were your responsibilities as youth worker?

To develop youth activities and have a major impact on the youth already in the church.

7.   Did you feel these were acceptable?

Yes, I think so. It was what I expected really. I think it was after the honeymoon period had ended that things kind of went downhill.

8.   What did your work actually involve, week to week?

I ran a youth Alpha course and After School Club, which I had set up within the first month. That was all I really had managed to set up before I left and the youth services, which happened once a month.

9.   How did your line management structure work?

I had a Youth Committee group, which was led by three older members of the congregation, which was helpful to have, but when the main person left, who'd been the one with all the vision for young people, this group then became pointless.

10.   Did you feel supported by the church leaders / members?

At first the church were really on my side, but once I started wanting to get out in the community and reach secular young people they all decided that they were not going to support me anymore, because that was unacceptable and they believed that I should have only been reaching church young people.

11. Did you feel that your time as a student at Cliff College sufficiently prepared you for your work with that church? Please explain

At the time I felt that Cliff prepared me for short-term missions, but not for full-time ministry. The missions were good, but they didn't provide realistic experience for life in full-time ministry, particularly with young people. I thought I'd done quite a lot while I was at Cliff in working with young people, but it was so incredibly different working as a full-timer, than just doing the odd ten days here and there.

12. Specifically, what did Cliff prepare you for?

Cliff was great from an academic point of view. I learnt a lot. On the practical side of things though, I'm not sure how valuable it was. I loved going on mission though, and doing them helped me to do certain activities – holiday clubs and youth events, etc.

13. And what do you feel it did not prepare you for?

It didn't prepare me for how to deal with people, for example managers etc. I do feel that if people are going to go into full-time ministry after leaving Cliff then maybe a few weeks actually working with a youth worker, or whatever area of ministry they feel called to would be of help. Just to have some idea of what's expected in that job. I know I would have really benefited from that.

14. Why did you leave this job?

I left because I had the feeling that the church had started to lose interest in having a youth worker. While I was in the job I had some personal problems too, which didn't help matters.

15. How do you feel Cliff could better prepare students for church-based youth ministry?

I think I would prepare students for the workplace. Helping them manage time, deal with people, learn how to set up programmes, but most of all making them aware of what a workplace is like and seeing if they feel that they could imagine themselves being part of that workplace and whether they could handle the post. Youth work is not just about understanding young people, it is about managing people as well, especially in full-time youth work.

I think the problem is that most students leave Cliff thinking that they will be ok in a church based youth work job because they know lots about young people. When you get out there and have to do a hundred and one things at a time, you tend to become a little disillusioned. I think the problem sometimes lies with the churches too. They tend to like the idea of a youth worker but don't seem to think the job description through enough.

At the end of the day a youth worker has to find 40 hours work per week in a job. What can you actually do for that amount of time every week when young people are at school?

16.   With the benefit of hindsight, are there things you would have done differently, either as a student at Cliff or as a youth worker?

I would have handled the whole situation differently now after being in youth work another six years after leaving my first post. My problem was the job itself. Though it all seemed fine at first, it wasn't what I expected it to be. I was inexperienced as well to be an overall leader. I know if I was in a similar position now, I would definitely have done things differently and acted more responsibly. I still feel called to youth work, but my first job was not right for me. It was just too big for me and I couldn't handle it. Now I could do it and I am aware of things you need to make clear at an interview to make sure you don't go into a job unaware of what you're letting yourself in for.

17.   Would you have benefited from some external support from Cliff during your first year in youth ministry?

One of the Cliff Evangelists was my mentor, and helped me a great deal. I phoned her many times to ask for advice. She was always a good support for me. I think it's really important to have someone you trust who's outside of your work situation who you can talk to, and ask for advice.

18.   Any other comments?

I think people leaving Cliff, or any college I suppose, are often in a rush to get a job. There's huge financial pressure for one thing, also there's a bit of a stigma about graduating with no job to go to. No one wants to be the one who's done three years at college and hasn't got a job. I know, looking back, that I rushed into getting a job. I knew I wanted to work with young people, but, as I say, I think that I actually went for the wrong job. I wasn't ready for it at that time. I wish I'd not been in such a rush. I'd definitely encourage Cliff students to take their time, and not just accept any job they get offered.

Also, Cliff needs to offer some proper careers advice. If this had been available when I was there, I might not have ever applied for the job I did. I think it's crazy that there's no careers advice structure at Cliff.

Interview VI: Graduate

Male
22 years old when graduated, previous employment experience

Currently in initial youth ministry post

Date: 10 October 2006

1.   How long have you been working full-time in church-based youth ministry?

Four and a half years.

2.   What is it about working with young people that motivates you?

I suppose one answer should be that 'I seek to do a good job for the Circuit which employs me' but I rarely feel that way. I am motivated primarily by two things: A desire to fulfil a call which God placed upon my life, and to see young people grow in faith – to have been a small part in the journey of faith of a young person and to see them in turn share what they have learned with their peers.

3.   What led you to apply for this post?

Responding to God's call, but not knowing where, I applied for several posts in different locations. I was offered this one, so I accepted. It was also possible at the time for me to commute from home rather than having to move house.

4.   Tell me a little about the church with which you work

My job is Circuit based for the Methodist Church. The Circuit has thirteen churches ranging from inner city to suburban (middle class). The age range is generally in the 55+ for most churches. Young people are present in every church, but are mainly concentrated in four churches.

5.   What led to them appointing a youth worker?

Cynically I would say that they needed someone to do the work which nobody was interested in doing. The circuit, as I understand it, looked for someone to advise, and to be involved in youth work around the circuit, to initiate youth ideas and lead youth services and weekends. In other words, someone to do everything with young people.

6.   What are your responsibilities as youth worker?

I have involvement with three churches, primarily, with a view to developing sustainable work among young people; work which can continue without the need for a full-time youth worker to be present to keep it running. My work also includes involvement in other activities which link to circuit work – two lunchtime clubs per week in a school, school assemblies and meetings.

7.   Do you feel these are acceptable?

Yes, since I developed them! I sought to change the way in which my job is structured about a year ago and focus work for a limited time in three churches with a view to moving on to other churches after a while. I found that working across the whole circuit was unproductive, and in some ways a waste of time.

8.   What does your work actually involve, week to week?

Youth clubs with Christian input, Uniformed Organisations – Campaigners, Girls Brigade and schools work – all weekly.
    Circuit staff meetings, Circuit leadership team, Circuit Meeting, Youth Management committee – all monthly.

9.   How does your line management structure work?

I am responsible to one Minister in the Circuit who acts as my Supervisor. I am employed by the Circuit meeting. My line management structure does not always work that well, as everyone thinks that they should have their say in what I do and how I do it, thus it all gets confused and everyone believes that I am accountable to them, when I am not.

10.   Do you feel supported by the church leaders / members?

Yes, by some. As a member of the Circuit staff team I am supported by the rest of the staff and there are some church members who support me. There are some though who are not particularly interested because I'm not the Minister. The youth worker / lay worker seems to be a second class staff member and thus not quite as important as the Minister.

11.   Do you feel that your time as a student at Cliff College sufficiently prepared you for your work? Please expand on this

No. Out of three years' study and experience, only a fraction was concerned with youth work, but since I had no idea where God was leading until I left, I can't really complain too much.

12.   Specifically, what did Cliff prepare you for?

I began to have a theological understanding of mission, of culture and of the nature of the church. I had ideas concerning programmed events for youth and children's clubs, assemblies and all age worship. It gave me some insight into understanding child protection issues; though I wish this important aspect of youth work had been taught / developed more with us at Cliff.

13.   And what do you feel it did it not prepare you for?

Conflict within churches. How can you work with a group that is unwilling to work together?
        Relational dimensions. I guess I wasn't prepared very well for this important aspect of ministry.

Church structure/Leadership. I had no idea really how to deal with volunteer staff who were under my supervision.

Coping when you don't particularly fit the perceived role and image of a youth worker. This is something that I kind of struggled with I guess. I think it's important to recognise that as a youth worker there's not one mould which all fit into.

14.   How do you feel Cliff could better prepare students for church-based youth ministry?

To experience youth work in many different settings for more than just one week or one day a week. To shadow a full-time youth worker and gain an understanding of all that goes on, not just the exciting stuff.

To be prepared to do some administration work, to recognise that all of the youth work does not involve direct contact with young people.

Understand how their denomination works and how lay employees fit into it.

How to use resources effectively – not always follow one book, but to pick 'n' mix a bit to make a suitable programme for the needs of their own group.

To find a support group and not to allow the employer to dictate who supports you – you must feel comfortable with the members of the group and be able to confide in them.

Ways to deal with conflict, parents, bullying, etc.

Networking skills.

I would strongly encourage students to continue reading books relating to youth work, but also not to view them as the only way to understand a context or to deal with a situation.

15.   With the benefit of hindsight, are there things you would have done differently, either as a student at Cliff or now as a youth worker?

As a youth worker, I would have developed the job into something workable much sooner. I continued to work at a job for three years which simply didn't work. If I had changed it all earlier it would have been more productive and useful to me and the Circuit.

16. **Would you have benefited from some external support from Cliff during your first year in youth ministry?**

A support group based at Cliff for those involved in youth work, would have been helpful I think. Particularly in terms of sharing ideas, resources, etc. The contrast between Cliff and the job was incredibly stark. I think I would have benefited from severing the link less rapidly, so having a group that met at Cliff would have been good. In some ways I needed somewhere to vent problems, struggles, etc. outside of my working environment. I didn't really have anywhere for this to happen, other than family and friends. A more objective group setting would have really helped.

17. **Any other comments?**

I wonder how much importance the Church places upon 'calling' when dealing with youth workers. Must a youth worker be called by God or must they simply be willing to do the job? Churches often employ people to be youth workers who are just not suited or called to youth work. Can Cliff be part of this discussion? Is there a way to offer churches' advice on appointments or to offer to be on interview panels? Often churches are looking for people with lots of experience in youth work, rather than theological training. In my opinion, it begs the question 'Is experience better than knowledge?' I personally do not believe that a person can be an effective church based youth worker and teach young people about faith in Christ, without some training in theology. How can the church be encouraged to value people for their gifts rather than their experience?

Interview VII: Graduate

Male
23 years old when graduated, previous employment experience

No longer in initial youth ministry post

Date: 17 October 2006

1.   How long have you employed in full-time church-based youth ministry?

In the church I worked for after I left Cliff, I was there for four years. I currently work for a large Baptist Church in which I am in my fifth year. I've not done anything other than full-time youth work since I left Cliff eight years ago.

2.   What is it about working with young people that motivates you?

A passion to see them come to know Jesus and to grow deeper in their relationship with God. Young people are often so energetic, inspiring and willing to get stuck in. They are fun, but also challenging. Looking back I wish I had had people who would have looked out for me and encouraged me in my faith, this motivates me to do this for young people, and purely a sense that this is what God has called me to do until he says differently.

3.   What led you to apply for the post?

A Cliff tutor gave me the advert and suggested I applied, at that moment something happened inside. God clearly spoke to me and said He was calling me into youth work. It all came together – the years I had spent leading youth outreach missions as a teenager and gaining more biblical knowledge at Cliff were all a training ground for this. It was the only job I applied for because I was certain this was where God was leading me to.

4.   Tell me a little about the church with which you worked.

It's an Independent Church and when I was there it had a membership of about 250 people. When I started the job there was a small core group of about 10 young people aged between 14-16yrs and about the same number between 10-14 yrs. The church itself was in the middle of an estate and was joined on to the side of the community centre so it was in an ideal location. The church at the time had an Anglican Minister and the worship was fairly modern and charismatic. I developed very close links with the local middle school taking lessons, assemblies and even running a mission at the school. There was also a Christian Schools trust that worked in the town. Myself and youth workers from other churches worked alongside this organisation and were involved in putting together many joint youth events.

5.   What led them to appointing a youth worker?

I think they saw the need in the community and the opportunities to reach out to the estate but also they wanted to see their own young people grow and develop in their faith and for them not to grow bored with church.

6.   What were your responsibilities as youth worker?

It was a two-fold approach; firstly to nurture the young people in the church and secondly to reach out in to the community. So I set up and ran a variety of things including Youth Bible Study meeting, an Alternative Worship event, Prayer meetings, Youth Club, After School Clubs, weekends away, summer camps, schools work and some detached work. With all these groups I was responsible for planning, running and determining the vision and development of them. I was also expected to clean and tidy the areas I used and make sure things were as the church expected them to be.

7.   Did you feel these were acceptable?

Yes. I always had a sense that I was serving the Lord first and in a way the Church second. I saw all my responsibilities, even the cleaning as setting an example for the young people to follow, a good role mode for them to emulate. Only occasionally did I have to attend things that were not directly associated with my job description – but that is part of being in a church. I never have seen my 'job' as a job I have always viewed it as a calling. This is my ministry and I will do whatever it takes to do it. I believe that means making the church that I work for 'my' church, making this my family, making the churches vision and mission mine, and that will sometimes mean being responsible for things I don't always expect.

8.   What did your work actually involve, week to week?

I have named some of the things above, but to try and put it in context; I would run the Bible Study, After School Club, Youth Club & Children's' Club every week. All these things would obviously involve preparation and resources. I would meet with other youth workers every week to pray and generally be together for support and encouragement.

9.   How did your line management structure work?

I was responsible to the Minister, then the leadership team, then the Church Council, and then the members.

10.   Did you feel supported by the church leaders / members?

Yes, I felt supported by different people in different ways, but when I was looking around the church during the interview weekend, I made sure that personally I would be happy so that meant me asking the question, 'Were there people my own age?', 'Were there people I would get on with?', 'Did I have a good rapport with the leaders and minister etc.?' All of that is important when it comes to feeling supported. I think support is a two way street, you have to play your part in the process and not just sit there doing nothing, then complain when you don't feel supported.

I always felt the Minister was supportive. There were times when we may not have understood each other, but he encouraged me in his own way and gave good advice on my leading and preaching. The church leaders were always very positive and would spur me on. I also set up my own support group from people who I got to know in the church. This group was specifically for me to share anything I wanted about the church, people, or whatever. It was completely confidential and I always felt that I could share anything. I found this group particularly helpful. I also had the support network of other youth workers.

I think I'd also add that whilst I always felt supported, the job wasn't always plain sailing. I had ups and downs, as with any job. I think too many youth workers expect their work to be fine and dandy all of the time. Life just isn't like this. You have to learn to take the rough with the smooth, and work through tough times, not just give up at the first hurdle. I've known quite a few youth workers who haven't really grasped this important aspect of ministry. There needs to be greater stickability from some youth workers. In my own experience, the most fruitful years of my ministry have been after four years in the same job.

11.   Did you feel that your time as a student at Cliff College sufficiently prepared you for your work with that church? Please expand on this

I did enjoy my time at Cliff, I know it where God wanted me to be at that time and don't regret going there. However, I would definitely say no, Cliff did not prepare me very well for full-time, church-based youth work. I often think I learnt negative lessons at Cliff – how *not* to do youth work, how *not* to treat people, how *not* to lead, and so on. Cliff, in many ways is so 'unrealistic' in terms of what life is like outside of Cliff. When you've been there for three years, you kind of become a bit institutionalised.

While I was at Cliff, the missions and placements were often very poor in content of what we actually did. Also the leadership of these teams were often very frustrating as often the leaders were in all honesty not very good. In three years of being at Cliff I can only remember two periods away, one a mission and the other a placement where I really saw good practice, and would say I learnt so much about how to do things, as opposed to how not to do things. Two positive experiences in three years is not great, I don't think.

12.   Specifically, what did Cliff prepare you for?

Cliff gave me the opportunity to learn more about God's word and to put the theological alongside the practical giving me grounding. It opened me up to a whole world of different theologies, ideologies and different opinions of God, church, leadership, and so on. This was all good preparation for ministry and helped me to understand how people think. I think my time at Cliff prepared me to get on finally with my calling and live the life God wanted me to. I was ready to leave when I did, but needed those three years. I naturally grew as a person and spiritually developed and discovered my strengths and weaknesses in that time. It was also the place where I developed some of my gifts.

13.   And what do you feel it did it not prepare you for?

I don't think Cliff prepared me for practical youth work. When I started my job I drew most of my examples from my experiences on youth outreach missions I'd been involved with before I went to Cliff. As I stated earlier, as much as I love Cliff College, as far as practical experience goes, I learnt more of how not to do things, than how to do them. It did not prepare me for different types of youth work or different types of young people; it also did not prepare me for the cultural differences that young people often come from.

It just all seemed a little superficial. Things that used to get me quite angry and annoyed at Cliff really drifted in to insignificance when I was in the real world of work. Maybe some of that has to do with my own personal growth, but things that were important to me at Cliff seemed less important when I was working. I guess it comes back to what I said earlier about becoming institutionalised at Cliff. You all kind of live in a Christian bubble that they call 'community'. It's great, but it really does make you lose perspective at times on reality, and on what's really important.

Many people who were at Cliff when I was there and left to become youth workers. In my opinion, at least half, though probably more, were simply not suitable for youth work. This was either due to not being gifted or having the wrong attitude, in other words, thinking they knew it all, had very high opinions of themselves or that being a youth worker was an easy life. I always felt that Cliff did not prepare people in this way, by being honest enough to say to people 'You are not right for this job.' Many people who were at Cliff at the same time as I was got full-time youth worker jobs, and then messed up. The best preparation for leaving Cliff would have been helping the students to understand or develop their calling. If this had been done in an honest and real way then perhaps people would have been less quick to jump on the youth work band wagon, and the people who were called and gifted would have been encouraged in this direction.

14. Why did you leave this job?

For several reasons really; firstly when I started the job the core group of young people were all either 13-14yrs old. By the time I left they were 17-18yrs old. I had had the privilege of being with them and investing time in them throughout their GCSE's and A-Levels, I had watched the main group grow and develop as young people and spiritually as Christians. As the majority were leaving to go to university it just seemed like the right time to move on and face a new challenge.

Secondly, the Minister was also going to be moving on the year after I left and so it just seemed natural for me to leave before this big upheaval. More personally, I had been married for two years before I moved on, but we both thought it would be good to start somewhere together, to both be in a new place.

Also I believe I had achieved a great deal in this time and had left a good platform for a new person to come in and continue the work I had put in place.

15. How do you feel Cliff could better prepare students for church-based youth ministry?

There should be more teaching about 'Calling'; what that means, how we know what our calling is, how we weigh it up with scripture, how we test our calling etc. Also I think it's important to give opportunity to actually test people's calling. We sometimes make the mistake of thinking that just because someone is gifted with young people that they are called to work full-time with them. My experience suggests this is not true. The opposite of this, though, is that those who are called will also be equipped to fulfil their calling and this will be demonstrated through their gifts. Teaching about calling would hopefully make people think about why they go in to youth work. Too many go in to it as preparation for the 'real' ministry, this is really annoying. Too many go in to it thinking it will be easy work until they decide what they really want to do.

There needs to be more teaching about practical youth work, but only to those who are called or testing a calling, looking at things like what the fundamental aspects of youth work are, working out a strategic vision for youth work in your context, how to deal with and get the best out of volunteers, what to look out for when applying for jobs, what questions to ask, what pitfalls to avoid, and much more. There should also be more teaching on leadership. I know Cliff does teach this and I found some of Howard Mellor's lectures on this helpful, but more in depth teaching on church based leadership is needed. Dealing with difficult situations, the qualities of a leader, how to train young people up in leadership, what to look for in potential leaders. Also enabling students to discover what type of leader they are, and how that will that affect the way they work. Although I am a youth minister I want to grow as a leader so I can better lead young people.

I also think there should be more teaching about character development too. I see many people leave Cliff with an arrogance which suggests they are amazing, that there is nothing more to learn. I don't blame the college for this, but this needs addressing. Things like developing a teachable spirit and character are vital to youth work, and all aspects of ministry in fact. Students should be encouraged to constantly learn from others who have been in ministry a long time. The whole arrogance thing needs addressing, in my opinion. I'm sure that's been the downfall of many youth workers, particularly those who have little experience; it's like they need to impress people all the time, when what they actually should be doing is admitting that they don't know very much, and start to learn from others. Being afraid to be vulnerable is a dangerous place to be, especially as a new youth worker.

Also I think the college should do more about how to stay spiritually fresh as a leader; how to stay strong in the faith and on the right path.

16. **With the benefit of hindsight, are there things you would have done differently, either as a student at Cliff or as a youth worker?**

Yes definitely, at Cliff I think I would have relaxed more, and not got so worked up about trivial things. I think I would like to have challenged the college more over the issues that annoyed me, not to make trouble but to understand their perspective and perhaps offer a new one. I may have made different decisions regarding third year placements and actively tried to develop my gifts more.

17. **Would you have benefited from some external support from Cliff during your first year in youth ministry?**

I think due to my experiences of youth work and leadership at Cliff I would not have benefited from support after leaving. Now that probably sounds arrogant, after what I've said earlier, but I honestly don't mean it that way. I think if I had been taught more of the things I suggested then support in my first year would be a much more natural thing but as it was when I left, I don't think it would have been of much help really.

18. **Any other comments?**

I think it's fair to say that Cliff is first and foremost a Bible College, not a youth work college. It can never prepare all students for all possible employment routes. I think students should recognise that if they want specific training, they should go somewhere that offers that training. Maybe they should go to somewhere like Oasis after they finish at Cliff if they want to be full-time youth workers. That would equip them far more, because that's the whole purpose of places like that. Cliff is more of a foundation place, in my opinion. The problem is after three years, people have often run out of money, and quite simply need to get a job.

Interview VIII: Graduate

Female
22 years old when graduated, previous employment experience

No longer in initial youth ministry post

Date: 2 November 2006

1.   How long were you employed in full-time church-based youth ministry?

Two years.

2.   What is it about working with young people that motivates you?

It makes me feels like I am doing something useful, using my gifts and changing lives.

3.   What led you to apply for the post?

Primarily the location. I had just got married and my husband had also just started a new job in the area that we were living in. Secondly, I had no idea what I wanted to do when I left Cliff but I thought it would be something I would be good at and definitely something I would enjoy.

4.   Tell me a little about the church with which you worked

I worked for a large Anglican church that was fairly modern with large congregations and four services each Sunday. I was one of four staff members – the Vicar, the Curate, the Administrator, and myself as the youth worker. The church catered for all ages and put lots of resources into growing and developing all that was happening there. There were lots of traditional elements about the church, a robed choir and old style communion services, but then there were also the youth services, the alternative worship and the many children's and young people's groups that met regularly. The church catered particularly well for uniformed organisations, and had the biggest Boys Brigade in Liverpool.

5.   What led them to appointing a youth worker?

Well, they said that it was because they felt that they needed someone to oversee all the youth work, but often I felt that it was because other churches of their size had youth workers and so they felt it necessary to have one too, even though the job was a bit vague.

6.   What were your responsibilities as youth worker?

It was all very vague from the start, to be honest. The job description was not clear and, as I had not worked full-time before, I didn't realise that this wasn't normal. I was in charge of 11 -18 year old groups. Some of these I acted as leader to and others I just enabled the leaders to lead. It was never really clear whether my role was to lead all the groups or just act as a resource. I think this grey area caused a lot of problems for me and the church because nothing was ever clear or defined. I didn't want to step on anyone's toes and vice versa. In the end I just did my best to build relationships with the teenagers and that turned out to be fruitful work.

7.   Did you feel these were acceptable?

As I mentioned before, the roles were unclear. I felt very unsupported by the staff and by the church itself in my job. The people there didn't know what my role was and didn't know how to use me. I was left to fend for myself and any new ventures or ideas I had were disregarded because apparently I didn't have the authority to suggest such things and carry them out, despite the fact that I was on the staff and attended weekly staff meetings. A comment after I had announced my resignation was 'You weren't what we expected.' So clearly something never clicked and I wasn't used how I should have been, despite every effort to make a difference. I worked very hard, yet had a negative experience.

8.   What did your work actually involve, week to week?

Weekly – staff meeting and lunch, early morning staff prayers, leading Sunday school groups, leading the Youth Fellowship, Youth Cell, Guides, Boys' Brigade, Youth Club, administration and planning, pastoral visits, After School Clubs, leading and preaching at Sunday Services.

Regularly, though less often – taking young people camping and on trips, organising the youth band, organising leaders meetings for each group.

9.   How did your line management structure work?

My line management was interesting. The Vicar was my boss (he had a wife and three kids, the youngest lad at home – he's a year younger than me) and there was the Curate and the Church Administrator. We would all meet on Mondays for staff meeting and then staff lunch. The Curate's husband would also come to the staff meetings. He was the Youth and Children's Co-ordinator, unofficially and unpaid. The Administrator was a long standing member of the church. Then we would all stay for the staff lunch which would include the Vicar's wife and the Vicar's son too. Often it would be a time where we would talk about church issues but mostly it was a time for the Vicar's wife to 'catch up' on church gossip! If something to do with young people was discussed, she would have her opinions and often take me to one side after lunch and tell me what she thought I should do. She often made me cry because everything she said undermined my authority and made me out to be stupid and incapable at what I was doing.

At every event I was organising she would keep up to date with what I was doing and put in her opinion about it. Every idea I had, I ran by the Vicar who was quite interested and agreed with me most of the time, yet when it came to the weekly staff lunch, his wife who really had no role in church would suggest in front of people that it wasn't a good idea, and perhaps I should consider doing it her way. She didn't do this because my ideas were bad, more that she wanted to be in control of everything that happened in the church. She didn't do it to me alone, but also to the Curate and the Administration Assistant. It was unfortunate, but she felt that she had to control everything and know about everything.

My line management would have worked far better if the Vicar had kept things with his family more separate.

10.   Did you feel supported by the church leaders / members?

Some of the parents really appreciated me, the kids did too. The leaders of the groups were very supportive but often I had to support them. I felt the staff to be unsupportive and I didn't feel that people wanted me there most of the time, or maybe it was just that they were too busy to care.

11.   Do you feel that your time as a student at Cliff College sufficiently prepared you for your work with that church?

In terms of resourcing me for youth work, my time at Cliff was very useful. I had many ideas from missions that I used again as a youth worker. It helped me to see the workings of a church before embarking upon a career there.

12.   Specifically, what did Cliff prepare you for?

I think it prepared me for life, in lots of ways. It didn't specifically prepare me for youth work but that's because I didn't do a degree in youth work. The disciplined life was good preparation for ministry in general as well, though it sometimes felt like nothing would be done anyway, if a person chose not to conform to the discipline at Cliff. I think it used to be much stricter years ago, that's what I've heard people say anyway. I also learnt loads about myself and my faith was both deepened and, at times, tested and stretched.

13.   And what do you feel it did it not prepare you for?

It didn't prepare me for relational tensions within churches and church leaders who don't seem to have any idea of how to help new staff, or recognise when the new staff member really isn't happy. The problem with being part of such a close knit community like Cliff is that in so many ways it's just not like real life. The support and close friendship with people is so much better, in my opinion, than in 'the real world'. It really felt like one huge happy family, most of the time. Of course there were people that rubbed others up the wrong way, but nothing like what I experienced in my job here. I guess that whilst that sense of community, security, support and friendship was wonderful, when it was gone completely, I didn't know what to do.

Also, the missions I went on were great, but they were too short to be of any real use in terms of preparation for church work. We were in a place we'd never been before, so the whole novelty aspect was a big deal. I mean, people are always nice to you when they don't actually know you, and even if they're not, we always knew that in just over a week's time we'd be leaving there and going back to Cliff. Working through issues and tensions with people was never part of the deal with missions. In my experience anyway, if there were any problems, the team leader would deal with them, not the students.

Also, the fact that we were always part of a team, I don't think helped to prepare us for life after Cliff. Certainly in the church work I've experienced, teams were nothing like as good as they were at Cliff. Although I was part of a staff team, I never really felt included or welcomed within that team. I know of lots of youth workers who don't even have a staff team, they're even more on their own with things. Looking back, I wonder why Cliff places so much emphasis on working in teams, when it's just the opposite when you leave and go to work for a church, whatever job you do – youth work, lay work, or whatever.

14.   Why did you leave this job?

To return to Cliff! I felt God was calling me out of a tricky job situation. I was no longer able to stand the critical Vicar's wife, and I felt that she had caused me to lose my confidence. I was held back there, I wasn't able to do the things I wanted to with the youth work; there wasn't a place for me there. I had felt like this the whole time I worked for the church. I left because I needed to feel peaceful again. The job had made me suffer with stress in a way I had never experienced before, and hope never to experience again.

15. How do you feel Cliff could better prepare students for church-based youth ministry?

Cliff should inform students that working for the church is very difficult. Unless your line manager or management group actually know how to manage people there is very little joy. There needs to be proper support in place. I didn't have anyone supporting me in my job. I would say to them the youth work bit is easy and rewarding, but the rest of the job is really tough.

16. With the benefit of hindsight, are there things you would have done differently, either as a student at Cliff or as a youth worker?

As a student I would have worked harder to get a better degree! As a youth worker I would have sorted out any problems with the Vicar's wife in the beginning, and not allowed the situation get as bad as it did.

17. Would you have benefited from some external support from Cliff during your first year in youth ministry?

Yes definitely.

18. Any other comments?

I definitely think I went into the job naively believing I would be ok. I never thought I'd have struggled as much as I did, or had the problems I had. The whole thing has made me much more cautious about working for the church ever again. I also think I was possibly too young and inexperienced for the job. If I'd have known what it was going to be like, I don't think I would have even applied for it. I think Cliff could do a lot more in terms of educating students about what life as a full-time youth worker, or lay worker is really like. I know I'm not the only one to have found things difficult, I've heard of lots of other ex-Cliff students who ended up quitting their jobs with churches due to negative experiences. It's a big problem.

Interview IX: Graduate

Male
25 years old when graduated, previous employment experience

No longer in initial youth ministry post

Date: 11 November 2006

1.   How long were you employed in full-time church-based youth ministry?

Six months

2.   What is it about working with young people that motivates you?

I think it's the sense of satisfaction that you get from seeing kids who go from not wanting anything to do with God or Church to becoming more involved, especially to the point of saying, 'Yes, I want to become a Christian myself.' There's a lot of joy in that.

3.   What led you to apply for the post?

I'd felt called to youth work for a few years really. While I was at Cliff I went on a few missions where there was a lot to do with teenagers. I really enjoyed doing this kind of work, especially with kids who'd gone through similar experiences to what I'd been through. I started looking for youth work jobs in my second year because I wasn't sure if I really wanted to stay on to the third year. In the end, I did stay for a third year and the job I applied for came up towards the end of that year. It just seemed right to apply for it, so I did and amazingly I got the job.

4.   Tell me a little about the church with which you worked

It was a growing Methodist church of about 160 members. They'd had full-time youth workers there before and the work with children and young people seemed really good. When I first started the job I thought I was going to love it. I quickly made some friends in the church; I was invited out for tea almost every night in the first few weeks, which was great. The problem was some people were always comparing me to the other youth workers that they'd known who'd worked there. That was quite hard. I'd never met these people, but it felt like I knew lots about what they'd done. Most of the things people said about them were good and felt like 'How can I ever live up to that?' Other things they said, about one person in particular, sounded really awful. I think I learnt what not to do from hearing what they had to say about some of the bad experiences they'd had.

5.   What led them to appoint a youth worker?

As I've said, the church had had a number of youth workers over the years, some were full-time, such as myself; some were part-time. I guess I was just the next one in the line. The woman before me had been doing the job part-time for about four years I think, but she'd left a year before I arrived.

6.   What were your responsibilities as youth worker?

I was never quite sure, to be honest. There was Sunday School, and I used to do the older group who were between 12 and 14. There was about 7 or 8 of them usually. There were a number of uniformed organisations that used the church building, though I don't think any of them were run by church members. I used to help out with them sometimes, mainly Cubs and Scouts. We had a Youth Club on a Wednesday night every week, where we'd play football and stuff. It was mainly lads that came to this group. I did a bit of schools' work, but not very much. The Head Teacher was not ever so keen I don't think. There was other general stuff that I did in the church – services, prayer meetings and so on. I also had to write, put together and photocopy the weekly church notice sheet because there was no one else to do it. It felt sometimes like they just expected me to be at everything, and do the stuff that no one else wanted to do. My responsibilities weren't really that clear to be honest. I had a contract and job description and stuff, but they always gave me the impression that I was expected to do more than what that stated.

7.   Did you feel these were acceptable?

Most of it was fine, it was what you'd expect a youth work job to be, but sometimes I'd feel guilty for having a day off and things like that. It was just little things that people would say that would make me think that they thought I should be doing more. I think youth workers are sometimes treated like general dogs bodies, who'll do anything and everything that gets thrown at them. There were times when I was not happy with what I was expected to do, and I didn't feel some things were acceptable or part of my job.

8.   What did your work actually involve, week to week?

On Mondays I went to the Mums and Toddlers Group held in the church. I chatted with the parents and grandparents who were there. This was never easy as it's hard to start talking to people at an event like that when you don't actually have a child there with you. I'd meet with my line manager on Monday afternoons as well, just to talk about how things were going.

On Tuesdays I sometimes had a school assembly to do, though not every week. Tuesday evenings there was a church prayer meeting that I used to go to.

On Wednesdays there was the Youth Club in the evening, and I'd be preparing things for that normally in the day.

Thursday I'd catch up on paperwork in the office, then Cubs and Scouts in the evenings.

Friday was usually my day off.

On Saturday I used to play football in the morning, and some of the older young people would come along to that normally as well.

Sundays involved doing Sunday School for the older kids, then I'd go to the evening service later on.

9.   How did your line management structure work?

I'm not sure it really was a line management structure at all. I'd meet with the Minister usually once a week and talk about how things were going. I never found him the easiest person to talk to though, so I don't think I was ever totally open and honest with him. I don't mean that I deliberately didn't tell him things; I just didn't feel comfortable about telling him how I was really feeling.

10.   Did you feel supported by the church leaders / members?

I think I did at first. As I've said, people were bending over backwards to be friendly to me. It was good for the first couple of months I guess, then I just got quite disillusioned with the job. I don't think my attitude helped though, to be honest. I ended up alienating a number of adults within the church I think. I guess I felt I should only really be working with the young people, so I wouldn't turn up to other stuff at the church if I could avoid it. I know that didn't go down too well. I think it all led to some people losing confidence in me and what I was doing. There were some good people there though, and I kept in contact with some of them after I'd left for a while.

11. Did you feel that your time as a student at Cliff College sufficiently prepared you for your work with that church?

Not really. I mean Cliff was a great place and I learnt a lot about the Bible and theology, but in some ways, that wasn't what I needed to know when I started my job as a youth worker. It felt a bit like I was in at the deep end, and had to either sink or swim.

12. Specifically, what did Cliff prepare you for?

Cliff provided me with a good foundation for ministry. I went to Cliff wanting to learn what authentic, effective evangelism really meant, and how I could be an authentic, effective witness to Christ's work in my life. I've already mentioned I gained a lot of biblical and theological knowledge. The missions were good, but in some ways were more like holidays. I don't mean they were an easy ride, but we were only there for a short time. We knew we'd be going back home to Cliff, and when you're with a team, it's a bit like a family. So I'm not sure how far the missions went in terms of preparation for work after I left Cliff.

One thing Cliff did teach me, which has remained with me ever since, was the whole spiritual discipline thing. As much as I used to hate getting up early to pray, I think that's been one of the most helpful things that I learnt there. I believe that discipline as a Christian is really important for any ministry.

13. And what do you feel it did it not prepare you for?

Looking back, I don't think I was prepared for the tensions that were there in the church where I worked. It often felt like I was in the middle of things, I kind of knew about stuff that was going on, but then people would be telling me other stuff that seemed to contradict what I knew. That was horrible. I wasn't prepared for that sort of stuff. There were loads of things that, looking back I know I just was not ready for, either personally or professionally. I know I made a lot of mistakes in the short time I was there. I definitely learnt a lot.

14. Why did you leave this job?

I realised the job just wasn't right for me. It wasn't what I thought it would be, I guess it was more difficult than I expected in many ways. I enjoyed working with the kids, but working full-time for a church is so different to being a volunteer, helping out. Also, I'm not sure youth work is something you can do long term. There will probably come a point where you're too old, and I guess it would be difficult to retrain in another career. I decided to move on rather than stay in a job I couldn't see myself doing long term and didn't really feel was right for me.

15. How do you feel Cliff could better prepare students for church-based youth ministry?

I think there needs to be more information on what to expect when you start a youth work job with a church. Also, although I'd done quite a bit of youth work in the past with my home church, there needs to be more information on what to expect when you start a youth work job with a church. It's very different to voluntary youth work or Cliff missions. I wasn't ready for it. I think Cliff needs to teach more about that sort of thing, maybe get people in to do some lectures on being a full-time youth worker.

16. With the benefit of hindsight, are there things you would have done differently, either as a student at Cliff or as a youth worker?

I think I would have looked into other kind of work, instead of just going for a youth work job. I might have been better at lay work or something more general. I think I went into youth work kind of with my eyes closed. As a youth worker, I guess I could have listened to people more, who probably knew what they were doing far better than I did. The problem was, like I said before, I didn't feel comfortable talking to the Minister about things, problems I was having, I guess admitting I wasn't totally sure what I was doing.

17. Would you have benefited from some external support from Cliff during your first year in youth ministry?

Yes, I think I would. I kept in touch with friends from Cliff, but that sometimes made things more difficult, because they all seemed to be doing really well and loving what they were doing. Maybe if one of the tutors had been in touch, or if I'd talked to one of them that might have helped. But again, I'm not sure I would have been totally honest about how things were going, even with one of them. You don't want to admit you're struggling do you?

18.   Any other comments?

This is the first time I've ever really talked openly about these experiences to anyone. It's actually quite healing just to voice some things. I guess I've kind of blocked a lot of things out of my mind until now. Even though I didn't stay very long in that job, I don't really regret doing it. It was tough in some ways, but I know I learnt a lot from the experience. To be honest, as much as I like working with young people, I don't think I'm called be a full-time youth worker, that's not where God's leading me. I still enjoy doing youth work, but not full-time, it's not me.

Interview X: Dave Edwins – On Track Ministries

Date: 26 July 2006

1.   What role do you currently play in the ongoing support of graduates?

When graduates leave and go into Christian ministry, many of them find they are not terribly well supported, perhaps the church aren't very well prepared for what they're doing, and often they need someone to come alongside them, care for and pastor them and so on. The role varies from person to person: with some people I have a mentoring role and see them four times a year, other people I would see intermittently and others it's more emails, telephone calls, etc. Sometimes people come and stay here as part of the ongoing support as well. There's really a whole range of things. It's being a listening ear for people who want to sound things out and feel that they don't really have anyone else to talk to.

2.   You mentioned that some churches aren't very well prepared for employing a youth worker, can you expand on that a little?

Some churches have a very clear picture of what they want. They know what their mission is, they know what their values of the church are, they know just the sort of person they want, therefore that person fits in and it's not a problem at all. Other churches I think are unclear and really don't know what they want. Do they want a children's worker?, a family worker?, a youth worker?, What's the brief? – Is it 0 to 18 they're going to be working with?, etc. So I think because of that they're pretty unclear often; all they know is that they need someone to help them because their young people are not involved in the church; they're losing them basically. So I think it's a lack of clarity and vision on the part of the church and the leadership of the church, and sometimes people are walking into quite difficult situations unknowingly and find themselves in 'out of their depth'.

3. **Some view the increase of churches employing youth workers as a reaction to the fact that there are fewer young people attending church. What are your views on this?**

A lot of churches are just aware that they haven't got any young people anymore, so they must do something – 'Oh let's employ a youth worker', but they haven't really thought it through. Rick Warren encourages the question 'What is the vision of the church?' In other words, 'What is the purpose of that particular church?.' Every church has a purpose obviously which is to glorify God, to worship and to witness. We know that those are the three key things. But then churches have then got to work out what God wants them as a church to do and to be involved in. And it may well be that they are to be involved more with older people rather than younger people, but they've got to work out who are the people we're supposed to be working with, what does God really want us to do. Not what's he doing with the church down the street, but what's he doing with us? And therefore I think they're unprepared and have not thought through fully what sort of person they really want, or believe is right for their situation.

I think within that as well, churches don't often think through what their responsibilities are. Churches have a responsibility to encourage, mentor and guide youth workers in what they do. Many churches haven't really thought about that at all.

4. **How long does your support of an individual continue, in this official capacity?**

We've only been doing it officially for two years now and so it's difficult to know. There's one guy I see and I see him three or four times a year in a mentoring sort of way and he very much wants it to continue, and I guess I'll continue until such time as he says it's time to move on. I think you realise sometimes when it's time to move on. For some people it's a very brief thing. In our first year we had a guy who had no support in his church and we went to see him and his wife probably three or four times in that year, but then he went into the

Baptist system and they wanted to mentor him as part of their system, and so therefore we were no longer needed and so have had very little contact with him. It really is a matter of what works for the individual. There's plenty of work to do, it's just finding the right opportunities to help people.

5.   Who instigates the mentoring relationship; you or the graduate?

I think it's a mutual co-operation and knowing when it's time to move on, and not being upset when that time comes. There are always other people who'll need help.

6.   How did this all come about?

I've been at Moorlands now for seventeen years, and in that time a number of students have left who we've had good relationships with, and they've been more like friends rather than student – teacher sort of relationships. So in a sense it's always been part of what we wanted to do, we enjoy doing it. Just keeping in contact and when they've gone through some tricky times we've been there to say 'what about this, why not this?' Not to tell them what to do, but to ask the right questions so they can think through what they should be doing. So that's been going on for a long time, but then three years ago we were on a church house party up in Suffolk, and during the worship, I felt like I'd been moaning to God and saying 'there are so many students that leave college and mess up because of all sorts of reasons – marriages have gone wrong, they've got on the wrong side of the church and are out of ministry. I'd been saying to God 'you've got to do something about this' and as clear as you and I are sitting here, God said 'Dave, *you've* got to do something about it. Don't moan to me about it, you've got to go out and do something about it!' I talked it through with Marian and we both felt it was the right thing to do, and was something we could do together. Eventually it meant leaving Blandford as well because it was easier doing the work from the base at college. So that's how it all came about. We felt very convinced that this was what God wanted us to do.

7.   Why do you see it as so important?

We train people at Bible College, we spend time and invest in their lives and I don't want to see people waste that, and we've been able to get involved and actually avoid that situation several times. I just want to see people succeed in ministry basically. Having put their hand to the plough, I want them to finish the race and complete the task God's given to them, and to keep going in ministry. I think it's really important for the health of the church and for people outside the church; I mean it must be such a bad witness to non-Christians to see people in authority in the church fouling up, whatever the reasons. It's just really bad news for the Gospel. There's a sense in which it can be terribly lonely in ministry, who do you talk to? Who is there to share with? You perhaps can't share with your colleagues because there are things that you wouldn't dream of sharing with them and you need someone outside of that situation who can be a separate voice, a listening ear, a sounding board or whatever.

8.   How do you relate to the graduate's church / leadership?

Well hopefully we'll be involved in the church leadership. In one case, we met the whole of the leadership, explained to them what we were doing and said that we were there for them as well as the graduate. It's not one sided. If the church has worries about the youth worker, then we like to be involved in those conversations as well to try and be of help if we can. Also, I preach at the individual's church at least once a year.

9.   How many graduates are you currently working with?

There are two churches that are currently funding us to spend time with their youth worker. There are a whole load of other people, some who support us out of their own money, but we've never formalised the arrangement, but we regularly go and see them. Others we have round for meals, if they're in the locality they can come to us more easily. There are probably about thirty to forty people we see every quarter. Some will be repeat visits, some will be one offs.

10.   Roughly, what percentages of those have left Moorlands in the last three years?

Probably 50%

11.   On Track Ministries is something that graduates 'opt in' to; are there support structures in place for those who choose not to involve themselves in On Track?

The key to all this is ongoing relationships. There are some students who we don't have a close relationship with during their time at Moorlands, and it's less likely that they will want to pursue an optional accountability relationship with us formally through On Track. Generally speaking they would receive support and similar mentoring from someone else, either connected to the Church they are working for, or outside of their work situation. Students are encouraged to ensure they have some sort of support group structure in place when they leave college. The constant problem with this is that some people are incredibly self-sufficient and independent and wouldn't ever want someone else to 'walk the road' with them, and certainly not want advice or guidance. It's an attitude of 'I know best, and that's the end of the matter.' Other students though, who have had some sort of prior friendship with Marian and I during their time at Moorlands are far more likely to want to continue the friendship and on going contact, and do actually want the contact to be more of a mentoring relationship than purely friendship based.

12. Do you feel that Moorlands graduates are adequately prepared and equipped for full-time youth ministry when they leave college?

I think we have an excellent, robust youth work course here, but of course I'm biased! In all seriousness though, we do everything we can to prepare students for all aspects of work with young people. We have a structure called SPAR – Spiritual, Practical, Academic and Relational. We work on those four premises throughout the entirety of the degree course. The relational aspect of the structure is really important, as it's often in this area where youth workers make serious mistakes, and ultimately end up dropping out of either that particular job or ministry altogether. Of course there is always more that can be done, and I'm not saying we get it right 100% of the time. Generally though, students leave with the tools they need for youth ministry, what they do after that in some ways is up to them. Also, there are always going to be glitches in character, and some people will mess up not because they've not been trained sufficiently, but just because of who they are, and unfortunately that does happen from time to time. And as a college we can't plan for that; when it happens, it just happens. We try to address those sorts of issues, but it comes back to the old saying of 'You can lead a horse to water, but you can't make it drink.'

13. Do you get sufficient support from Moorlands in your work with graduates?

Yes, although there's no financial support whatsoever; we get a good level of support and encouragement from the leadership and staff of the college. They are definitely committed and see the value of what we're doing. It's been something of a different matter with the College Board of Directors. In today's society of litigation, if we give advice to someone and then they do something drastic – commit suicide for example, then there's the concern that somehow that may have implications for us. (On Track) There are all those sorts of fears in people's minds in taking some sort of responsibility for people after they've left here, and I kind of understand why the Board are a little bit wary about the whole thing. We've actually joined a professional association for teachers which provide indemnity cover because we realise that there are risks in doing what we're doing, and some people sadly abuse help that's offered. Generally speaking though, we get a lot of support from the college, but the fact is that it's a new venture, and some people are often sceptical about anything that's new. We also practice what we preach, in the sense that On Track Ministries has a support group who we are accountable to and who keep us in check. This is really important, so that effectively we don't go off the rails in any way. We can't talk to other people about accountability if we're not accountable to people ourselves.

Interview XI: David Firth

Level Three Course Director

Interview concerning vocational advice available to Cliff students

Date: 16 January 2007

1.   To what extent are Level Three students advised/guided concerning career paths?

The process involves various course meetings, group tutorials and individual tutorials. There is a general session that looks at how to prepare a CV, preparing for interviews – putting together a presentation, going prepared with sensible questions, etc. Also there are sessions where students are made aware of career options available to them once they have graduated. The various graduate recruitment websites are shown to them and explained. These websites are very helpful to the students, and a number of students have been inspired to pursue a particular career after seeing the variety of options available to them. These all happen in the second semester, usually in the February of their final year. The problem with doing these sessions so late in the course is that by this time most of them have already worked out what they want to do when they leave Cliff. I believe we need to develop these sessions within all three levels.

2.   In your opinion, is this current system adequate?

I think the actual content of what we do is fine, it's just needs introducing much sooner within the three years. The other thing that I feel needs to be emphasised from an early point is that studying at Cliff, or any theological training institution doesn't necessarily have to lead to ordained ministry or church based employment. There is a vast range of career paths open to theology graduates in secular employment, which can often provide more opportunities for evangelism than working in a church. Often church based jobs – lay work, youth work, etc involve working with mainly Christians. The secular workplace however is often a great place to engage with non-Christians, in a way you may never experience in a church based job.

It raises the question 'What is ministry?' There are many people who work in teaching, or industry or commerce or whatever who say 'Actually I feel called by God to do this job.' Surely that's just as much part of ministry as it is to work for a church.

3.   How much emphasis within these sessions, discussions is placed upon 'calling'?

It's important to recognise that some students come here already sure of what it is God is calling them to do, and they've come to Cliff to get some training for that. Most, if not all students by the time they get to Level Three do feel some sort of call upon their lives to something. So we're working from a base level of 'I feel called to....' We explore in group sessions the question 'What does it mean to be called by God?' The more specific aspects of call, i.e. 'I feel called to be a youth worker' are looked at in one to one sessions, where their gifts, abilities, motives, and so on are discussed in some depth.

4.   In what ways do you think Cliff could improve on the way students are guided concerning their future work/ministry?

As I've previously mentioned, I think we need to incorporate this teaching into Levels One and Two. Also, in our recruitment advertising and promotion, we should be emphasising that a degree from Cliff can lead to a wide variety of employment options, not just Christian based work and ministry.

Interview XII: Extracts from Sally Nash Interview

Director of the Midlands Centre for Youth Ministry

Date: 23 January 2006

What Bible colleges do that perhaps youth specific training institutions aren't able to do is to root their training in spiritual and ministerial formation.

Often youth workers who are still quite young themselves, are often very good at relating to the young people they are working, but not so good at relating to adults, and this often results in problems which can escalate. Also, many churches have high expectations concerning youth workers, disproportionate to the expectations they have concerning other ministries in the life of the church.

Something that often occurs, particularly for youth workers who haven't worked full-time before going to college, is that they simply don't know some of the basic elements of doing a full-time job. Again, this can contribute to poor working relationships and escalate into much larger problems. A theme that's prevalent in education is concerning empowering students to be autonomous learners, taking responsibility for themselves and, although it's important to encourage this, I think perhaps we need to be more pro-active in making some things clear about what is expected as an employee. It sometimes works the other way as well and we find that some youth workers are doing too much, risking burnout. There does need to be more said about this within training programmes.

I think one of the benefits of the JNC status is that, where a church based youth worker's situation changes, and perhaps they feel they want to move into statutory youth work, if their qualification has professional status (JNC) then this is possible. Whereas if they've worked in church based youth work, even for a number of years, without the JNC recognition, it will be much more difficult for them to get a job within statutory youth work. Also, it helps dialogue and general working together with those involved in statutory youth work. I also think the aspects of youth work taught within a JNC recognised course incorporate a lot of good practice. That's not to say that a person is less likely to be professional if they don't have the JNC, but there are just a lot of benefits to having that status.

Bibliography

Books, Journals and Associated Research

Appleby J & Appleby D, 'Surviving as a Youth Worker' in
  Perspectives: Surviving as a Youth Worker, (summer 1998)

Black W, *An Introduction to Youth Ministry* (Nashville, Tennessee:
  Broadman and Holman Publishers, 1991)

Blaxter L, Hughes C & Tight M, *How to Research* (Buckingham: Open
  University Press, 2001)

Board of Education and Board of Mission, *Good News for Young
  People: The Church of England's National Youth Strategy*
  (London: Archbishop's Council, 2002)

Bonhoeffer D, *Life Together* (London: SPCK, 1985)

Borgman D, *When Kumbaya is Not Enough* (Peabody, Massachusetts: Hendrickson Publishers, 1997)

Bosch D, 'Vision for Mission' in *International Review of Missions* LXXVI No 301, (January 1987)

---, *Transforming Mission: Paradigm Shifts in Theology and Mission* (Maryknoll, New York: Orbis Books, 1991)

Bowyer P, *Express Community* (Milton Keynes: Spring Harvest Publishing Division and Authentic Media, 2004)

Bowyer P & Bowyer R, 'A Practitioner's Experience' in *Perspectives: Believing and Belonging*, (autumn 1999)

Brierley D, *Joined Up* (Carlisle: Spring Harvest Publishing Division and Authentic Lifestyle, 2003)

---, *What Every Volunteer Youth Worker Should Know* (Carlisle: Spring Harvest Publishing Division and Authentic Lifestyle, 2003)

Brierley P, *Reaching and Keeping Teenagers* (Tunbridge Wells: Monarch Publications, 1993)

--- (ed), *UK Christian Handbook Religious Trends No. 6* (Worcester: The Trinity Press, 2007)

Campbell A, 'Youth Ministry: Profession or Calling?' in *Youthwork* (December 2006)

Christian C, 'Christian Youth Work Management' in *Perspectives: Surviving as a Youth Worker*, (summer 1998)

Clarke D, *Breaking the Mould of Christendom* (Peterborough: Epworth, 2005)

Clarke P, *Together in Mission* (Calver: Cliff College Publishing, 1994)

---, *Why Do Many Recent Former Cliff Students Leave Lay Worker Posts Early?* (Cliff College: 2000)

Cray G et al, *The Post-Evangelical Debate* (London: Triangle, 1997)

Croft S et al, *Evangelism in a Spiritual Age* (London: Church Publishing House, 2005)

Croft S, *Ministry in Three Dimensions* (London: Darton, Longman and Todd Ltd, 2000)

Davies R, 'Christian Youth What?' in *Perspectives: Christian Youth What?,*(spring 2005)

Dean KC, *Practicing Passion* (Grand Rapids, Michigan: Eerdmans Publishing Company, 2004)

Dean KC, Clark C, Rahn D, *Starting Right* (Grand Rapids, Michigan: Zondervan Publishing House, 2001)

Edmondson C, *Fit to Lead* (London: Darton, Longman and Todd Ltd, 2002)

Ellis J, 'Youth Work and Evangelism – Can They Co-exist with Integrity?' in *Perspectives: Surviving as a Youth Worker*, (summer 1998)

Fenton P, *Someone to Lean On* (Bletchley: Scripture Union, 1998)

Fields D, *Purpose Driven Youth Ministry* (Grand Rapids, Michigan: Zondervan Publishing House, 1998)

Fields D, *Your First Two Years in Youth Ministry* (Grand Rapids, Michigan: Zondervan Publishing House, 2002)

Fuller W, 'The Church and its Mission and Ministry' in Sookhdeo P (ed), New *Frontiers in Mission* (Exeter: Paternoster Press, 1987)

Furlong M, *The C of E: The State It's In, The Past and the Present* (London: SPCK, 2006)

Gelder A and Escott P, *Profile of Youth Workers,* Churches Together in England Co-ordinating Group for Youth Work (London: Private Report, 2003)

General Synod Working Party *Youth A Part* (London: Church House Publishing, 1996)

Green M, *Evangelism Through the Local Church* (London: Hodder and Stoughton, 1993)

---, 'Youth Work with Qualifications' in *Perspectives: Christian Youth What?*, (spring 2005)

Griffiths S, 'Christian Youth Ministry' in *Perspectives: Christian Youth What?* (spring 2005)

Ingram G and Harris J, *Delivering Good Youth Work* (Lyme Regis: Russell House, 2001)

Jamieson A, *A Churchless Faith* (London: SPCK, 2002)

Keats D, *Interviewing, A Practical Guide for Students and Professionals* (Buckingham: Open University Press, 2000)

Kolb D, *Experiential Learning* (Englewood Cliffs, New Jersey: Prentice-Hall, 1984)

Mason J, *Qualitative Researching* (London: Sage Publications, 1996)

Maxwell J, *Developing the Leader Within You* (Nashville: Thomas Nelson Publishers, 1993)

Mayo B, *Gospel Exploded* (London: Triangle, 1996)

---, 'Training Youth Workers at Theological College' in *Anvil*, 15/4 (1998)

---, 'Young People as Theologians' in *Perspectives: Young People as Theologians*, (spring 1998)

McLaren B, *More Ready Than You Realise* (Grand Rapids, Michigan: Zondervan Publishing House, 2002)

Mellor GH, *Cliff More Than a College* (Calver: Cliff College Publishing, 2005)

Mueller W, *Understanding Today's Youth Culture* (Wheaton, Illinois: Tyndale House Publishers Inc, 1999)

Nash S, *Supervising Youth Workers* (Cambridge: Grove Books Ltd, 2006)

---, *Sustaining Your Spirituality* (Cambridge: Grove Books, 2006)

Nel M, 'Why Theology? It is Only Youth Ministry' in *Journal of Youth and Theology*, 4/1 (2005)

Newbigin L, *The Gospel in a Pluralist Society* (London: SPCK, 1997)

Payne G & Payne J, *Key Concepts in Social Research* (London: Sage Publications, 2005)

Race P, *The Lecturer's Tool Kit* (Abingdon: Routledge Falmer, 2004)

Richards S, *An Exploration of the Notion of 'Sense of Vocation' Among Christian Youth Workers* (University of Oxford: Unpublished PhD Thesis, 2005)

---, 'Vocation and Christian Youth Work' in *Perspectives: Who's Calling? Whose Calling? (spring 2006)*

Riddell M, *Threshold of the Future* (London: SPCK, 1998)

Senter M, *Four Views of Youth Ministry and the Church* (Grand Rapids, Michigan: Zondervan Publishing House, 2001)

Shepherd N, 'Soul in the City – Mission as Package Holiday: The Potential Implications of a Tourist Paradigm in Youth Mission' in *Journal of Youth and Theology*, 5/2 (2006)

Shorter A, *Toward a Theology of Inculturation* (Maryknoll, New York: Orbis Books, 1988)

Spencer N, *Beyond the Fringe, Researching a Spiritual Age* (Calver: Cliff College Publishing, 2005)

Strommen M, Jones K, Rahn D, *Youth Ministry that Transforms* (Grand Rapids, Michigan: Zondervan Publishing House, 2001)

Vernon M, *Pastoral Care for Young People* (London: Marshall Pickering, 1997)

Ward P, *Growing up Evangelical* (London: SPCK, 1996)

--- (ed.) *The Church and Youth Ministry* (Oxford: Lynx

Communications, 1995)

---, *Youthwork and the Mission of God* (London: SPCK, 1997)

Wright W, *Mentoring* (Milton Keynes: Paternoster Press, 2004)

Wright W, *Relational Leadership* (Carlisle: Paternoster Press, 2000)

Websites

http://www.mayc.info/section.asp?id=1153

http://www.nya.org.uk/Templates/internal.asp?NodeID=90814

http://www.youthwork.co.uk/community/Forum/boardindex.asp

Cliff College Validation Documents

BA in Theology Course Approval Paperwork (Cliff College: 2004)

Collaborative Partner Report (Cliff College: 2003)

Diploma in Youth Mission and Ministry Course Unit Outline (Cliff College: 2004)

Evangelism and Young People Option Course Unit Outline (Cliff College: 1999)

Revalidation Portfolio (Cliff College: 1999)

Printed in the United Kingdom
by Lightning Source UK Ltd.
129324UK00001B/78/P